MINDING OUR MANORS

MINDING OUR MANORS

—

JOHN GOODYERE

© John Goodyere 1983
Privately published 1983
Printed by
Biddles Limited, Guildford, Surrey

Text and cover design by Humphrey Stone
Woodcut by Robert Tilleard

ISBN 0 9508996 0 7

Distributed
by Element Books
The Old Brewery, Tisbury, Salisbury
Wiltshire SP3 6NH

In Memory of Frank Sykes

Contents

	INTRODUCTION	1
	THE WORK	3
1	The Landowner Today	5
2	To Plant a Tree	21
3	A Green and Pleasant Land	29
4	Bricks and Mortar	39
5	An Old Saw	52
	THE DIVERSIONS	63
6	Household Gods	65
7	Adding to the Hoard	75
8	A Garden of Delight	85
9	'Of Books there is no End'	92
10	The Chase	109
11	A Bloody Massacre	121
	CONCLUSION	127

Introduction

These essays are about life in the country written from the property owner's point of view. There is much talk about the nation's rural heritage these days but little mention is made of landowners and the part they play. They are the people responsible for its maintenance and upkeep. Their views and notions are rather different from most of the euphoric outpourings on the subject. They have a wealth of experience but their views are not entirely acceptable to an increasingly egalitarian world that grants nebulous freedoms over anything that might take its fancy; hence the very phrase 'our rural heritage' which is, of course, just work to those who look after it.

Such things are only worth having because the owners have been to great trouble and no little expense to make them so. These owners pay substantial taxes and many share their fading glories with the public, so no one can say they are a selfish set of people but their views are rarely made public, or when made so, may not prove very palatable.

Times have changed a great deal in this century for property owners and I want to show how they have reacted and adjusted to the new circumstances. Naturally I fall back on my own experiences and describe the informal system of management I have devised, a system in which the landowner gets quite dirty but emerges with his dignity intact.

Likewise, I tell of the various amusements and pastimes

of a countryman. I feel more fun can be had on and off a property than many people know of; I also touch on the various intellectual palliatives open to a person living in remote rural areas. These are very different from those available to a townsman. For instance the library will take precedence over the theatre and the idiosyncratic results are shown here; this is why your foxhunter is reading books and the village handyman lecturing on literature.

We have to go out of doors in all weathers and know the countryside to be a battleground between the cultivators and nature's uncontrolled verdure. However lovely a vast and quiet landscape may seem on a summer evening, we do not forget the days of rain and fog, the mud and even the 'nails that Dick the shepherd blows'.

I shall also discuss in some detail what landowners do, their relations with their tenants and society, especially the latter because it has changed so much within one person's lifetime, causing a crisis of spirit within the landowning classes. They belong to the rearguard of our civilization, dragging behind them a great rag-bag of the past; their houses, the old furnishings and portraits, not to mention any number of old fashioned notions that are not quite without merit. I like to think that this caudal appendage serves to balance the body politic and restrain the wilder fancies coming from the other end.

There are some who will argue that every vestige of this older order should be swept away; not unnaturally, I think otherwise and whatever specious arguments may be put forward, there is no better defence for Mr Wilkins in his Surbiton villa with his rights and freedoms than a landowner in his historic house, as the latter, an obvious target, receives the first attack.

JOHN GOODYERE

THE WORK

One
The Landowner Today

The historian G. M. Trevelyan, writing of the landowning classes of the early nineteenth century, said that they lived a life 'more completely and finely human than any perhaps that has been lived by a whole class since the days of the free-men of Athens'. This is heady praise from one born amongst their numbers but of sufficient intellectual eminence to be impartial. The modern observer is tempted to look around and see what is left of such a praiseworthy body of men. He will have to look quite hard because the remnants are maintaining a low profile, as they say in military circles. The observer, having sighted his quarry, will also want to consider if the remnants are worth preserving. I can assure him that they are still there, shorn of their political power and much of their wealth, going through the motions of being the ruling class and having an undercover dab at a bit of power even yet.

I will look at these remnants and describe how they function. This will not be a plea for the reconstitution of the landed interest as it was before the First World War and Estate Duty, nor will it be a Messianic call to the survivors so that they might gird themselves up and come out of their rural fastnesses. I am biased of course, naturally wishing for their survival and I hope to indicate in what directions they best serve the common good, although there is much dispute about what that might be. Many will doubt that a privileged and historical curiosity has any part to play at all.

An historical resumé is necessary to set the scene. The Big Bad Barons of the Middle Ages went out with the Black Death and the Wars of the Roses. Under different titles they were partly revived as an institution by Henry VIII's largesse on his dissolution of the monasteries and proved haughty and contentious subjects. At the same time smaller proprietors flourished and began to develop into that numerous and homogenous body of country squires that had the making of the realm in the seventeenth and early eighteenth centuries. The curious need only turn to the pages of Fielding and other novelists of the period, to read of their doings and way of life. Towards the end of the eighteenth century the haughty barons re-emerged into prominence, buoyed up by money gained from the Industrial Revolution and better management of their estates. At the same time the more rustic and decayed families began to lose ground, disposing of their properties to the haughty lords or to the self-made men of the Industrial Revolution.

It was a time when the rich grew richer and the poor more numerous and the process continued until the 1870's, by which time the small 'one village squire' was becoming rare. More and more of England belonged to a small clique of landowners. The situation was unbalanced and easily overthrown, first by the failure of harvests, secondly by falling rents following the introduction of cheap corn from overseas, and thirdly by taxation aimed at reducing blatant disparities of wealth, a notion so outrageous at the time that many old families suffered a crisis of the spirit rather than the purse and gave up before they need have done. These blows were followed by the First World War with its enormous casualties, especially in a class that willingly 'went

THE LANDOWNER TODAY

over the top' first, waving their swagger sticks as they fell, never to return. Hard on this came the economic difficulties of the inter war period, another bloody war and our decline into a power of no great consequence. And yet, they are still there, battling on and, in some cases, not doing too badly either.

Their work is in two parts, duty and the management of property. The word duty has a good old-fashioned ring about it, not out of keeping with the subject in hand. This duty is being a figure-head and leading. Leading is not always pleasant and usually means that you are shot first and fed last. Landowners are supposed to be leaders because they are the descendants, real or imagined, of the old system that prevailed for eight hundred years from the early Middle Ages. In those distant days you had to be clever, rich and physically strong to maintain your position. You were not necessarily very nice. Civilization has tempered these things for the better but the demand for leadership survives and exceeds the supply, hence the demand for Figureheads. They need not be very animated; common-sense and honesty are enough. Their duties range from being church-warden to Lord Lieutenant. In between these two extremes lie innumerable activities to do with schools, charities, politics, councils, sport and the yeomanry. All of these have to have chairmen, committee members and such like. What could be better than a local landowner, a rock of financial security in a sea of shifting tradesmen; furthermore he can be trusted to take an impartial stand on difficult issues.

Attending interminable committee meetings is very dull, although as Chairman you have a captive audience as a consolation. In a county the fount of honour is the Lord Lieutenant and he is the Sovereign's local representative.

THE WORK

From this over-worked functionary spreads a great fan of minor patronage, public spirit, kindnesses done and repaid, all directed towards various good causes. It has been likened to back-scratching and permeates the whole fabric of society.

It works like this at a Church fête meeting; a committee member thinks he can get Lady So-and-So to open the fête. He will ask her and report back. He does not tell the other members that he ran a successful field day for another concern dear to the heart of Lady So-and-So's husband. In due course she comes and opens the fête, purchases a set of pink, crocheted doylies and a bag of currant buns, laughs at the rain and a few more people are drawn in through the gate to look at this other worldly visitant. It is a benevolent and slightly ludicrous way of doing things but good results come in and it works after a fashion that I would hesitate to improve upon. This sort of informal and unwritten code is typical of any balanced and healthy community but falls down badly in the great urban sprawls of this country. I do not mean the small towns, but have in mind the larger industrial places where so many people are brought together that it is difficult to leaven them with community spirit.

It is a hard world short of leaders. A few clergymen and doctors labour under great burdens; even the ogre-like mill owner has disappeared to some distant and cosseted suburban ghetto. The fate of these towns no longer hangs on the heavy gold aldermanic watch-chain taut across a portly buttoned affluence and this is not a bad thing as they do seem to have been dreadful at times. Occasionally in the past that Victorian figure of fun aped his betters seen on nearby country estates. Perhaps some good came of it, even if he only learnt that there were values not based on hard cash.

THE LANDOWNER TODAY

Politics is a useful field of endeavour for a landowner. Do not forget that this country achieved considerable eminence when they had the sole management of both Houses of Parliament. Things have changed and landowners are unpopular because, by the nature of the beast, they represent the traditional elector, a steady sort of fellow, rather than the shining idealist. This gets them a bad name with half or more of the people in the country but they do have one great recommendation: they live and work in the constituency as well as having considerable local influence. This is a great help in representing the electors whatever their political complexion.

The party that usually elects landowners has, of recent years, unwisely veered away from this sort of member preferring a more thoroughly professional-type of person, often having no more connection with his constituency than a week-end cottage purchased after his election. Nor is a landowner likely to be chasing extra money in enterprises outside Parliament, enterprises of a doubtful nature at times.

Back-scratching and public works are no substitute for a rent roll. They are only possible after receiving the rents, so a landowner's first interest must be his estate and the work he has to do to keep it going. Here he has three main occupations; farming, forestry and land-agent. For the smaller landowner, to turn farmer is his best hope of survival. Many have wisely taken this course and have become big farmers instead of down-at-heel squires.

New legislation has strengthened the tenants' security unto the second or third generation and so landowners will find it harder to take farms in hand when tenants die. By the same Act of Parliament the supply of farms for tenants has dried up for ever, creating a privileged class of farmers in semi-perpetuity. The larger landlord cannot hope to farm all his ground; farms do not come that large and this is a good thing because the farmer, be he tenant or otherwise, is an important part of the hierarchy in a balanced community. A village with a farming landlord that has lost half a dozen tenant farmers will be a poorer place with a gap in the middle.

Landowners on poorer soil and in hilly country are much occupied with forestry. The regular blocks of conifers are not loved by the amateur landscapists loose in the countryside today in such large numbers. I like a deep, dark coniferous wood but this is a personal taste and not widely shared. Forestry work is planned in a very long term rotation and the taxation is so complicated that it is understood by very few, and the officers of the Inland Revenue are not always amongst their number. Forestry is also subject to arbitrary and ill-considered changes by politicians who know that only country men grow trees and that their votes are too few to bother about. We must admire the faith of those who still persist in the folly of planting for their descendants; it is the massive impudence of this that causes offence, a positive rejection of social innovation, backed with hard cash.

Of course, the main occupation of a landowner is to be his own agent, if he thinks he can get round the work himself. Too often in the past the agent was a tweedy pre-war pastiche of his employer, the pendulous wealth of his plusfours sweeping the grass like a spaniel's ears, an impressive figure. Behind him, the careful observer might have noticed a person rather like a game-keeper or clerk of the works. This was his employer. These luxurious and alas, sedentary agents may be necessary on a large estate, but elsewhere they come between the landlord and tenant,

THE LANDOWNER TODAY

erecting an unnecessary barrier between them. To be one's own agent is the most natural and proper thing, enabling the development of a personal relationship of great delicacy. To take without offence and give without seeming patronizing is difficult. This is one of the most important things about good proprietorship because tenants must occasionally feel that the landlord is sucking the whole community dry. If the rents are known to be placed on horses or spent on high living, this impression is justified. As it is, much of it goes to the Inland Revenue. Fortunately that greedy behemoth has contrived rules that favour the return of what is left to effect repairs and maintenance, so one way or another the bulk of the rents get back to the community from which they are drawn, especially if the landlord is resident and spends his rents locally.

I hope I now have those amongst my readers who are landowners; sensibly dressed, resigned to only two days sport a week, be it pheasants, fox, fish or the turf, aware of their responsibilities and not pretending it is the year 1900. Now we can go to work, work is tenants and tenants are humans.

A landowner has a mild but not officious responsibility towards his tenants and since he usually lives amongst them, he might as well do so in harmony and friendship. If he cannot achieve this because they poach, steal Norway spruces at Christmas time and smash gates with their cars, then his community is unbalanced, probably by the spectacle of his excessive affluence and over-comprehensive management of the property – management that seems interfering and petty. The solution lies in the landowner's own hands as I shall hope to show.

A landowner has in his estate a microcosm of society. The dictionary describes a microcosm as a 'world in miniature' and this is just what a healthy village community is. In the village where I live this is borne out by statistical evidence. Our figures, drawn from two hundred people and multiplied by the necessary quarter of a million to equal the national population, conform accurately to the figures given for disease, mortality, money, church-going, car-ownership et cetera. That these two hundred people should conform so well makes me feel all is well with the community, no glaring vices rampage through the body politic of this village. We are an average community.

I feel partly responsible for this state of affairs because I have indulged in 'social engineering', a horrible expression to aggrandize the game of playing with people. To do this without burning your fingers requires a measure of lofty detachment or cynicism rather than the earnestness of the do-gooder, he being doomed to disappointment by the vagaries of human nature. There are quite a large number of people afoot engineering today. Most are civil servants or clergymen. Sociologists, you will be relieved to learn, only talk about it. This meddling with people's lives sounds an impudence, which indeed it is after a fashion. But it is very hard not to do good turns if it is easy, and good turns usually involve meddling in somebody else's affairs.

A landowner has the choice of who should live in his houses. He does not run a council-style, first-come, first-served selection. There is not a whit of impartiality in his choice. He can, should he feel so moved, descend on a deserving young married couple and endow them with a house, something they desire above all else. It is obvious that he who chooses the people who live in the village, has the moulding of the community in his hands. That is as far as a landowner need take his social engineering, so it is not quite the bogey it sounds.

THE LANDOWNER TODAY

A landowner is constantly approached for houses by all sorts of people. His first concern is his own staff. After these come his retired staff (Yes, people still do house them!). Farmers are responsible for filling their cottages and that constitutes the bulk of an estate's stock of homes. Farms and estates employ less people than they did formerly and so there is a surplus of houses. Many landowners sell off these unwanted houses, needing the cash or finding letting not very profitable.

These houses are often bought by people outside the community, who, while not necessarily devoid of community spirit and other virtues, need to be 'digested' before they become absorbed into the community. Often they are retired and so cannot play their full part. In short, they can become a burden and the delicate balance is upset. A village next to mine has changed completely – it is all Chiefs and no Indians. The natives that survive have retired to council estates, and only foregather in darkness at the less genteel public house.

On a country estate the surplus houses are best let to self-employed workmen or the natural increase of the village. By following this policy on my own property we have a blacksmith, a family of builders, two carpenters, two general contractors and a person that fixes motor cars. A hundred years ago all these people would have been on the estate payroll. Now they are their own masters but are naturally pleased to undertake work in their own village and do so at a reasonable rate. The result is the same, but everybody is independent and happier as a consequence.

I take a Russian view of the business of proprietorship, as described in Gogol's 'Dead Souls'. In that now-vanished world the worth of a property was reckoned not by its acreage but by its people, their numbers, quality and docility. Land in Russia was limitless and readily available, but quite useless unless you had people to work it. I have no wish to transpose the habits of that expansive age onto our crowded island but the fact remains, clear and writ large, it is the people who matter.

A fat rent roll drawn from an unbalanced and hostile community is doubtless an excellent commercial proposition but it is no fit place to live in. Nobody wishes to live near a commercial proposition any more than they would like to live next to an ironworks or a plastic gas-cape manufactory, so it behoves a landowner to share out his good luck amongst the community for if he does not, the Inland Revenue will do it for him in a clumsy and unattractive manner.

I appreciate that any plea to reduce the very high rents prevalent on some estates will go unheeded by the owners of those properties, but these high rents have certain disadvantages. The rent of a let farm controls the capital value of the farm and, with capital taxation increasing and becoming due on sale or transfer, the passing on of farms to descendants is becoming harder. Very naturally the tenants demand a high standard of maintenance, higher than they would enjoy if the property was their own. A tap has but to drip and they telephone the estate office for a new washer to be fitted. Not only does this require a plumber but a secretary for answering the telephone and so the labour force grows in the manner so well described by Professor Parkinson. Due to the structure of taxation a landowner can plough back his rents in improvements and achieve thereby some tax relief. These improvements are often necessary but can be overdone. Rents can be increased as a result and a vicious circle is contrived from which the Inland Revenue alone draws the benefit.

THE LANDOWNER TODAY

In the informal and more modest system that I favour, the landlord, aided or prompted by occasional secretarial help, should collect his own rents. This delicate business of creaming off some of the surplus cash in the community requires considerable tact and good manners and it does no harm to either party if the landlord calls personally like any other tradesman who sells a service or goods. This intimate contact will help remove the landlord/tenant relationship from the emotive plane and put it beside the butcher and baker where it belongs. The landlord and tenant might even get to like each other and little harm could result from this.

For rent collecting, it is wise to strike an attitude much like that of a person making a charitable collection; a take-it or leave-it attitude that disguises the powers of coercion that do exist but about which it is good manners to say nothing. Diffident, yes, but apologetic, never; for that would cast doubts on the validity of the operation. Instead of getting one hundred pounds for a good cause out of the village, the landlord may be asking for twenty thousand pounds for himself and that self may not be very edifying.

Being seen to return much of the money to the community, the inevitable lot of a resident and conscientious landlord, does much to justify the large amounts of rent that can be collected: a known taste for selecting winners on the turf would have an opposite effect. The bulk of this money comes from farmers who are usually quite well off, despite the wails of the Farmers' Union. They have properly run businesses quite capable of producing the rent and if they cannot, then who is to blame except the person who chose them as tenants.

A smaller portion of the rents come from the cottages and as I observed earlier, these are no gold mine. The money comes in little bits and the occupants, when crossed, can be truculent. They are also protected by a great deal of legislation made necessary by indifferent landlords in the past. The weight of these laws is so great that it has now almost killed off the very thing it set out to protect, but the wisdom of some legislators rarely extends beyond the next polling day, so this is not surprising. A large clutch of cottages needs sensitive management. Tenants cannot always pay the rents. Sympathy in place of bludgeoning is much better in these cases. My own rents are roughly the same as council house rents and I have tenants who have troubles, yet there is no build up of arrears despite the provision in the rent books of a special column.

All these fine ideas of a gentle life in the country, everybody living in harmony, are best suited to the smaller estate. It is harder to arrange these scenes of rural bliss on a large property. The landowner cannot hope to know all his tenants so well; his greater wealth alienates those who cannot accommodate themselves to such a disparity of worldly goods. He cannot expect their sympathy nor can they hope to attract his. Of necessity he has to have land agents, clerks of the works and such like between him and the tenants. As a consequence he has to be particularly careful not to cause offence. It is best for this type of landlord to go 'institutional'. By this I mean that he should try to become like a revered institution, benign and God-like, undertaking various public duties like being a member of the House of Commons (though this is not always possible), or a Master of Foxhounds, so he is constantly in attendance on the public in the village halls and fields of his county.

Let me describe an ordinary day in the life of a landowner small enough to have to fend for himself. I draw from my own experiences.

THE LANDOWNER TODAY

Before eight o'clock I am rung up from a public telephone box by a tenant on his way to work. He informs me that last night's rain came in badly and fears that my bedroom ceilings will come down – a subtle identification of our joint interests. Will I come and look? I agree to do so after breakfast and collect the nearest long ladder available. He is quite correct, rotten battens and slipping tiles on the windward side had caused the leak. The roof had been getting worse for the last year or so. I nudge the tiles back into a more waterproof arrangement with a stick, standing on the top of the ladder and then promise his wife that I will rebatten and felt the roof in the summer. Nearly two years rent gone there.

My next call is on the Goodenough family, looking for small arrears of rent. I am informed that 'Dad's out and so is Mum. She'll be back later but Dad did say that the toilet cistern is flooding'. It is, and the loo doctor strikes again, bending the ball valve arm another half inch downwards. I return, penniless and wet-cuffed for my pains. I later call on Mrs Snodgett to see if her drains are working properly. They have been troublesome but are alright now, but then it is not Saturday evening, the chosen time for such troubles.

Having made these calls I can exercise my horse. This is not strictly work, but affords a time to see things and think. It also induces one to hang gates properly for there is no incentive otherwise. There are two hours of the morning left and I work at taking old fences down from around the woods. This is a very much harder job than putting up new ones since huge skeins of intractable wire are weighted down with rotten fence posts. I bundle them into heaps in readiness for a bonfire on a drier day and go home for lunch.

My next chore is to ring up for the rabbit clearance man,

having seen too many white scuts out riding in the morning. After lunch I look in on the builders working on some farm buildings but a natural lull seems to be asserting itself before they tackle a nasty part of the job. I lead the attack and make a reasonable showing, then retire after an hour or so with the job well under way. I pass the Goodenough home on my way back to see if Mum has returned. She has but has no money and suggests Friday evening for my next call. There is just enough time to make it worthwhile to resume my fencing work and I carry home a selection of old fence posts for firewood. It is tea time.

That is a typical day; much rushing around, plenty of physical work, good home cooking and fresh air, meagre intellectual stimulation, doing things for people that would otherwise be left undone – and yet rents are still called 'unearned income'!

Today, I have been a tiler of sorts, builders' foreman, rent collector and fencing contractor; tomorrow I shall have to be a stockman, forester, office worker and drive to the builders merchants to get materials.

More is expected of a landowner than a fast-moving decision-taking handyman. He is expected to be a community leader, a role I am not very keen on as I believe I blow down enough people's necks in the course of my work without doing it in the council chamber as well. This role of community leader comes from the good old, bad days long ago; when men wrestled to a prominent position by being clever, ruthless and physically dominant; a gathering of talents which would not find favour today.

Landowners are the descendants of these bad barons and are expected to play their part in councils, committees and suchlike. The withdrawal of services and amenities from rural areas has caused increasing dependance on handy

THE LANDOWNER TODAY

figureheads should there be any left. In our village, our school has gone, the sub-postmistress is ninety-two and will not be replaced, the rector lives in the next-door village, and retires soon, and he in turn will be replaced by one who lives in the next but one village. The shop has closed, its inadequate premises having prevented it from serving a wider field than just the village and so prospering. I am not anxious to be the next institution to fizzle out. Should I do so, I hope my going will not be as dramatic as that of the landowner in Laurie Lee's 'Cider with Rosie', where the whole village appears to have died shortly after its proprietor. The soul went out of it, if we are to believe the author, and I see no reason why we should not.

Nowadays, sharing is the key to successful proprietorship. I do not mean that a landowner should distribute the deeds of his estate amongst his tenantry, as this leads to people painting cottage doors yellow in their first flush of independence, and that would never do. A landowner is constantly approached by his neighbours for a vast number of favours that cost him little or nothing; things like firewood, fields for beanos, corners of scrubby grazing for ponies, the right to tip rubbish, park cars, exercise dogs and go hang gliding. All these are best assented to, not so that the landowner can hold the community in thralldom but just to oil the works and quiet the innuendoes of those champions of the underdog found in all communities – for no Aunt Sally is easier to hit than a landowner whose property is all over the place at once and consequently very vulnerable.

If you are the sort of landlord who 'prinks' about in flamboyant plus fours, my preaching will be far from welcome but the time has come to change a little. It was fun acting out a Wodehouseian pastiche of country house life, but the part must not be overplayed. England has a greater tolerance of fools and oddities than other countries, but at the same time we know how to compromise. Foreigners even envy our skill in this direction. We dodge the guillotine and with a little ingenuity we will avoid the red revolution, but to do so we must not be so sunk in our folly as to miss the moment of change. Each portion of the community has to adjust itself now and again to accommodate its neighbours. Twice, in 1832 and 1910, a blind wave of obfuscation overcame the landowning classes and caused a serious constitutional crisis, and twice we have crept on tenterhooks round the brink of the abyss. Now is the time to do away with the purple check in our tweeds.

Two
To Plant a Tree

For the serious forester the last decade has been dreadful. Long summer droughts have killed countless new plantings, Dutch elm disease has destroyed whole settled landscapes, taxation changes have mystified and deterred woodland owners, costs have increased, especially in fencing, which is one of the largest expenses and even the rabbits seem to multiply. I live on the chalk where I cannot hope to be a serious forester, and while all these troubles afflict me in some measure, I nonetheless plant for pleasure and enjoy myself. By removing the profit motive you recreate the leisured attitudes of our eighteenth century forebears and in doing so raise forestry, that rather drab and slightly discredited profession, to better things. 'Planting for posterity' has a sanctimonious and superior ring about it: your descendants or even the casual passer-by will be enormously gratified should success attend your efforts. It is not difficult to improve by planting the drabbest stretch of country imaginable and recently, with the loss of the elms, huge areas have been revealed as dull, characterless expanses.

I have always liked Stourhead gardens in Wiltshire, laid out in the eighteenth century by Mr Henry Hoare of that place, embellished and nurtured by his descendants and finally secured for the nation through the National Trust. I like it despite the rhododendrons, about which there are

THE WORK

two schools of thought and much hot debate; many enjoy their garish splendour, let them, but for my part I side with the original designer and being on chalk where rhododendrons do not grow at all, I can go about my own Stourhead without them.

To make your own Stourhead sounds an ambitious and lengthy scheme, which indeed it is, but I have the advantage of a valley much the same shape, surrounded on most sides by varied and disorderly woods ranging from dignified and mature clumps of beech to rubbishy bits of hazel and brambly undergrowth. These woods and a naturally good site surrounded by the high chalk downs are the raw materials for my plans; the work is half done already.

Such woods as I have are the result of two things. Firstly, in days gone by much of the steep downland slopes were given over to growing hazel which was used for firing, hurdles, laths, baskets etc.; it was one of the basic raw materials for rural life. The natural regeneration after cutting is rapid and as it was cut piece by piece in strips from top to bottom of the slopes, self sown trees had a good chance to grow up in the newly cleared pieces: these coppices were fenced with living hazel on their edges, laid like a proper hedge; this kept out the modest stocking of sheep in the past. The second factor was an early Victorian landowner in these parts, who for no obvious reason landscaped the hills around with clumps of beech, planting strips of the same trees at the foot of the hills: his house was over the hill a mile away, so I can only presume he did it for the sheer love of the countryside. Maybe he at one time thought of building another house here; he never did and I am lucky enough to live in a house built since amongst his planting.

Trees do not live for ever and these early nineteenth

century trees are now past their prime; every winter gale leaves an ugly hole in a clump or belt and so over a period of years I devised an adaptable plan of planting. My idea was to make good the gaps in the circuit of trees round the valley and introduce more variety by removing the superfluity of ash and hazel, encouraging beech trees and an evergreen element by planting holm oak, one of the few oaks that grow on chalk. To put real heat into the autumn colours I have planted Norway maple, a close relation of my favourite tree, the hated sycamore, loathed by gardeners on account of its fecundity, and disliked by gamekeepers for its destruction of pheasant cover, yet still prepared to grow willingly anywhere, which, on the chalk downs is a favour not to be despised. My Victorian forerunner placed great faith in the Norway spruce and a sorry mess they are a hundred years later, stunted, slow growing and unsaleable. For the necessary vertical element in the plan I am relying on Serbian spruce, a similar tree, happier on this soil. I do not favour the introduction of exotics; a startling effect can be achieved by using trees from China or Chile but the result is not an English wood, it is an arboretum and the consequences of indiscriminate planting for the sake of a different second name in Latin can be seen at Stourhead and many other such places. It is very easy to be tempted by nurserymen's catalogues but the enormous vivid fruits are consumed by the birds long before they make a show, the fiery autumn tints of exotics need an Appalachian climate which I have not got. These snares and delusions may have their place in the carefully nurtured woodland garden, but are out of place in large scale work. My effects are to be enjoyed at a quarter of a mile, not at the end of my nose.

My plan does not entail enormous planting; one well placed tree can go a long way to altering the appearance of a huge expanse of empty downland. The area involved is some 200 acres visible from the valley bottom; of this only 50 acres, mostly on steep slopes, is my share for planting, the rest is devoted to agriculture, an activity usually expunged from this type of undertaking. I have to consider the farmer's feelings; he is very long suffering and allows me to nibble a corner here and there and has learnt to rely on my fences round the woods to help keep his sheep where they are meant to be. Furthermore I rely on the farmer to provide an element in the composition that is very important at Stourhead, but quite unobtainable in a dry chalk valley, namely the lake. His fields of barley in the valley bottom are an economical and even profitable substitute for a sheet of water; no burnished mirror of classical antiquity ever reflected so accurately the changing seasons.

Stourhead lake is surrounded by a whole family of temples, every gurgle in a grotto sports a nymph or a demigod. For myself I recall the poet's lines –

> Worship one God only
> For who
> Would be at the expense of two

preferring Clough's terseness to Pope's rather flaccid versification at Stourhead. So it is that I have built only one temple and that stands in a clump of trees in the centre of the valley: I flatter myself that Stourhead's island is as yet unadorned. My temple is made of stone and concrete; the pillars were taken from a country house nearby, the cornice I made of concrete as the original was too heavy for me to handle; it is four pillars wide and two deep, the centre pair at the back being joined by a curtain wall with a seat beneath. Above the seat is the date in Roman figures (cumbersome as the 2nd millenium is approached) and my own initials, an excusable vanity as I built it myself. The floor is yellow gravelled and the whole building surrounded by sycamores that planted themselves in the clump after the original trees died. It faces towards my house half a mile off and every morning when I get up it gives me pleasure. Any bad details in its construction are fuzzed by distance and the sun lights it up very well. This pleasure was not always the case because when I had first finished it I was overcome by the sweat and toil involved and could only view it as a feat of ingenuity (possibly misplaced) or an exercise in construction. These feelings have worn off and I can enjoy it like anybody else's temple now! There are many sides to this enjoyment. Firstly the achievement of building something substantial, for it is not a contrived little garden nonsense. Secondly I enjoy imagining myself as a diminished descendant of the eighteenth century magnificos, playing around with the very last bit of classical sentiment afoot in this modern age. Then there is using it, not of course as a temple as I am well satisfied with the established facilities for worship already available in the village, but as a place to sit in and it is remarkable how the countryside is framed and improved by a row of pillars; it is broken into easily assimilated bits for enjoyment. It is much favoured by animals; pigeons and barn owls roost in it, deer rub off their velvet on the sandstone pillars in preference to my trees, mushrooms grow in the gravel of the floor. It is an excellent object for a short walk from the house and the picnic becomes a reliable pleasure once it gets indoors again.

As I have said, Stourhead has too many buildings and not enough open spaces. The original designer could not envisage how much his planting would grow or that later generations would be anxious to do their little bit by way of putting in many more trees and shrubs. I sympathise but regret this overcrowding; the eye must be able to rest, just as in architecture the correct balance between voids and masses must be sought. I would, however, much like to build some more nonsenses. Their charm is that they are small and have no use, so the imagination can do what it will; also being small they are easily realisable. I once had in mind a Chinese pagoda at the top of the downs on the edge of the woods with a cutting in the trees below it, allowing a vista of the temple in the valley bottom framed by branches. First I resorted to a book on Chinese architecture by Oswald Siren which showed me that the genuine article is either vast beyond belief or like a demented teapot. I returned therefore to the European tradition of chinoiserie and designed an economical but fussy conceit of light yellow brick coigned with dark blue engineering brick three diminishing stories high, each one punctuated by frills of glazed green pantiles cocked up at the corners with dragon-like hip irons from which are hung bronze bells with wind-moved clappers, all sufficiently lofty to be out of reach of the British boy. Such is the stuff of dreams!

Meanwhile, I hope to concentrate on the planting and fencing, so completing the circuit of trees about the valley and providing a track within it the whole way round, rising here and falling in another place, allowing sudden glimpses of the views. One of the difficulties here is the fencing which is always expensive but especially so where long thin strips are planned, a great deal of wire surrounding very few trees. Proper forestry fencing is beyond my pocket, so I plant a larger and more robust young tree than is normal in forestry; these, I grow myself. They can at least be seen amongst the nettles and undergrowth from first planting, for nothing is more frustrating than searching long grass for tiny trees, only to cut them down by mistake when clearing the weeds. Although it is considered best in forestry to plant very small stock, such schemes are only devised by those who do not have to weed the young plantations.

Besides beech, holm oak and Norway maple, in my limited repertoire there are holly, box, wild pear, plum, wild cherry and the incomparable whitebeam, all to be encouraged. Some I scrounge from neighbours' woods, taking young trees that have no chance to grow on account of the shaded places where they sprang up. The planting is done in the most arbitrary manner, trees being put in wherever and whenever I can get to them, so in this way I can be more sure of achieving the happy chance of nature, so much admired in our native woodlands. I am a pessimist and so rarely plant a single tree of a type by itself. Block planting is the answer and by putting in 20, 2 may survive to achieve the desired effect; the other 18 are victims of sheep, cows, horses, hares, rabbits, squirrels and boys wanting whippy sticks.

Why, you may ask, do you insist on meddling with nature in a place where she has done you so well already? Can you not leave your woods alone without labouring after the rather contrived effects you have described? To which I would answer that Man, and I am no exception, is a meddlesome creature full of various aspirations and ambitions, while nature, like good home cooking, is excellent in many respects but can be dull unless well spiced and varied. Were I to leave my woods strictly alone they would degenerate into a mass of poor quality ash and hazel. Of this sort of wood there is no shortage, profit or any great pleasure. I am reminded of the story of the clergyman extolling God's wonderful bounty as he surveyed his well kept garden; 'A fine mess it was when He had sole charge'

THE WORK

replied his gardener. It is wrong to curb such talents or inclination you may have to improve the world around you.

These are my plans for my own Stourhead, a prospect of many years work to be grafted onto a fortuitous arrangement of woods and pasture. I am not rushing at it, plant a bit here, fell a bit there; and with time will come discretion. In tree planting mistakes become evident only very gradually, but are easily eradicated. My only sorrow is that there are few to appreciate it with me for whatever I do, it will look like a lot of mixed woodlands and nothing else. And why? Because there are no rhododendrons!

Three
A Green and Pleasant Land

I am not the first to tell of the charms of farming, nor shall I be the last, because the whole business is becoming more pleasant every day as machines take away the drudgery. In classical times Horace, Virgil and lesser writers constantly sang of the pleasures of the field. How much real work did they do? Very little, I expect, and that little was light; hitching up their drapes, they may have ambled forth in the cool of the day to trim a vine or two, but no more. Toil, plain and unlimited, entered not into their scheme of things and I believe their enthusiasm was only a condition of poetic euphoria induced by watching others work – well known to be a satisfying occupation in itself. During the Renaissance and after, the theme was taken up again, pastoralism became a prevalent literary vice; bogus shepherds only laying down their pipes to mouth eternal verities. These contrivances remained in fashion until the end of the eighteenth century and we see their last expression at the court of Louis XVI where his queen played at dairy-maiding.

It is not surprising that the theme died, for at this time farming changed from a haphazard affair with occasional surpluses into a business proper. This occurred first in England where the matter was put on a proper footing and the regular surpluses went to feed the burgeoning masses of the Industrial Revolution. In order to achieve this, the extent and tedium of farm work was increased and the rural swain, so loved by the poets, was turned into Hodge the chawbacon, an object of pity whose paltry lot was justly championed by William Cobbett. The farm labourer was ground into an unattractive condition by over-work and about as much food as would make a poor school lunch for a child today.

How did they survive you may ask? They did not; they died young, though not before they had reproduced themselves. It is remarkable that so useful a class of person, doing such important work in healthy conditions, has been now nearly extinguished. The village in which I live, a very agricultural one by modern standards, has only eight farm labourers and three of these would be considered superfluous by some farmers: their employers could get by without them, though to the detriment of their life-style; by this I mean that they would have no time to have any life outside their farm. The end is in sight for the paid farm worker except on very large farms; modern farm methods have eradicated most of the ghastly toil and with this gone, so has the need for a large work-force. If a farmer can breed up a son or two like he used to breed his cart horses, then his problems are solved. This is why I said that farming is becoming pleasant again; no longer need he dread the five bushel sack. As for the farm worker, we shall miss him; no job nowadays offers such variety, calls out so many skills and is done in such pleasant circumstances. The survivors are far removed from the nineteenth century rustic and if their employers have any sense, are handsomely reimbursed for their pains.

Needless to say, I have been a farmer, as well as other things, but I am not one now for, despite singing its praises, I was not very good at farming. I do not think anybody could have gone about the matter in such a haphazard way. The failed farmer is a rarity these days: rising land prices and security of tenure have kept all but the most incompetent in business. My trouble was that while I had the land, I had not got the capital to work it or the knowledge of how to work. I was not lazy, my efforts were just ill-directed and intermittent. I did not understand that steady application was the answer to most problems; this virtue I only acquired in time to see the money run out entirely and a kind neighbour, an excellent farmer, told me I would make more money letting somebody else do the farming, which good advice I took and have benefited from ever since.

My farming was simple. I grew corn, using a contractor for all the operations; all I had to do was arrange the work and wait for it to be done; at harvest time I would step forward and collect the golden flood of grain. Despite even my erratic methods, the quantity of corn produced was too much for me to handle, nor did I have anywhere to store it satisfactorily; farming friends helped, but they had their own affairs to attend to as well as identical floods of golden corn. The real flaw in the system was the contractor. His combine harvester started ten miles away and worked through the farms towards me. I just happened to be at the end of his journey.

It was not, I must add, the contractor's fault; he was honest and hardworking, but I was still at the end of the line. My only consolation was that he never left me to go elsewhere, as is sometimes the wont of contractors. I remember that in my last disastrous season as a corn grower, he finished on November the twenty-second with two combines in darkness picking up badly laid corn already cut with a grass mower.

Disenchanted with corn growing, I started to keep sheep

towards the end of my career as a farmer. This is what I should have started doing when I first took up the trade. Things went better for me here, as I had great potential as a dog and stick farmer. No one knew better than myself how to lop an elder bush to fill a hole in a hedge. This side of my farming prospered, but did so too late; my modest capital was exhausted – even the Inland Revenue could bear my losses no longer, and so I finished with few regrets, leaving farming to those born and bred to it, which is not a bad thing.

I keep a few fields in hand for horses, ponies and a small flock of Jacob's sheep for the table. These evasive piebald steeplechasers of the ovine world are more interesting than the commercial off-white sheep. They enjoy better health than the ordinary sheep, being free from footrot; neither do they lie upside down and die trapped in that position. Their lambing occurs naturally without my assistance, and so it is that I can deny them the mollycoddling given to ordinary breeds. Natural selection works itself out in my flock and the sturdiness of the breed is maintained. But they do get out when the new grass comes in and bother my neighbours, and these I recompense with a leg of lamb at slaughter time. No amount of barbed wire entanglements will cramp their ingenuity, but unlike other sheep they are easily returned. I open their field gate and get to the far side of the errant flock, then I clap my hands and the wanderers, their faces visibly suffused with guilt, run back into the field. On the other hand, removing them from their home field is very difficult and needs as many people and dogs as possible. They lose their herd instinct and go to pieces, running in all directions except the one required.

Each year I forget the trouble that they make in Spring when the glut of meat comes in Autumn. We eat twelve lambs a year in our family and it is 'noisettes d'agneau aux fines herbes' all the way rather than a couple of chops girdled with fat and gristle. Here the sheep has a great advantage over the cow in that it is all good quality meat; skirt, sticking and shin have their place but it is not in the roasting oven.

That is the extent of my farming. The experience was, and is, very valuable, especially now part of my job is to be a land agent of sorts and this means keeping an eye on farms and farmers. The farmers I am responsible for are quite capable of looking after themselves without my meddling.

A land agent's main concerns on a let farm are buildings, gates, hedges and general tidiness. Farm buildings can cause trouble because they rot at both ends, standing as they usually do in a sea of ordure, navigated only by enthusiastic lads on tractors, and they none too careful at times. Gates are almost too expensive to erect; machinery is always getting wider and so a well-hung gate is a nuisance long before it is worn out. Hedges have to be cut, and cut properly; when looked after they are a very cheap fence, especially now when even a small field can cost several hundred pounds to make stock-proof. Modern machines make hedging easy, but the landowner's job is to put in a plea for any young hedgerow timber coming on. This must be a great nuisance to the cutter, but who else will try and save it? As to tidiness, I have been told by some that this is no part of a land agent's work but I do not like to see fertiliser bags, derelict machinery and corrugated iron lying about, even if only because they frighten and cut horses. What a boon the horse is in preserving rural England!

And the farmers themselves? They come fat and thin, mean and generous, thousand acre corn barons and twenty acre higglers. Yet no portion of the community is so level headed and consistently reasonable; I think this is so because they are doing something infinitely more worthwhile than most people; never a doubt enters their minds in this respect. As I have said elsewhere, the work is varied, healthy and done in a pleasant place. What more could a person want? The middling-sized farmer is the luckiest; he can have time off and some money to spare, yet enough work to keep himself fit and out of the office. At no great cost he can avail himself of the sporting amusements of the countryside in a manner that far richer people cannot afford. Yet he is often far richer on paper than those people who aspire to shoot or hunt beside him, but this wealth is tucked out of reach in his land and stock; the first cannot be stolen or lost, while the second constantly reproduces itself, given care and attention.

On the small farm, those described as uneconomic by agricultural authorities, the work can take up too much of a man's time. Keeping fifty cows on fifty acres is profitable but unless bolstered by considerate and similar neighbours, relief milkers and good contractors, it is a penance and a muddy one at that.

On the larger farms, say, six hundred acres or more, there is little scope for the farmer to get dirty. Much as he would like to get out into the fields, he cannot; the desk, the telephone and appointments call him back. My neighbour, the one who rightly suggested I should give up farming and let somebody else do it, farms over two thousand acres and is as desk-bound as an accountant. At the height of the harvest he is allowed to drive the combine at lunch time. Sometimes I see him riding the drill at sowing time for a breath of fresh air and I don't doubt that he looks over his stock when they are handy, but it is not farming as people

A GREEN AND PLEASANT LAND

imagine it; it is a business and much like any other. Another feature of these larger farms is that they have staff and a foreman, and should these people stay about the place they develop a routine and the farm almost runs itself outside the office. The farmer gets bored or adventurous and seeks other outlets for his energies; one will become a politician farmer on the National Farmers' Union, another expands into making dried grass-nuts for cattle feed, while a third will take a mastership in his local pack of foxhounds.

A farm is not like an ordinary commercial enterprise, it cannot run aground and be shipwrecked by six months of mismanagement; years of inattention leave it only slightly less valuable than it is when in good condition. Why should this be so? There are two reasons. A vast supply of would-be farmers and a limitless demand for land. Farmers are on to a good thing and know it. In times past small portions of the community have held the nation in thrall; the coal miners have done it in recent times and soon the diminishing world food surpluses will place the farmers of this country in a similar position of power. I hope they will be responsible with this new-found strength, the like of which they have not had since the 1870's. The record of the landed interest was not to its credit then, as it controlled both Houses of Parliament, held on too long to a policy of dear food and paid the penalty of sixty years in the doldrums. Now they only control one House, and that the least effective, the other being pledged to cheap food even now.

Not only is the food cheap, it also happens to be nasty and farmers feel disgruntled about this state of affairs and lay the blame, with some justification, on the politicians and the food processing industry. In the House of

Commons there is an important party that picks up no votes from the farming community – maybe just a few misguided 'two-churners' in the Welsh hills. This party has a lot of support from the eaters of cheap food although these same eaters spend a very modest amount on their victuals compared to many European countries, favouring those foods with the least good and most wrapping in their make up. It is no wonder then that farmers feel disgruntled with this anomalous state of things: one of the advantages of being a farmer is that you come by a lot of good quality food and know instinctively how to avoid rubbish. Nor is it surprising that a wholesome staple, when laboriously converted into something else, wrapped, advertised and humped from one end of the country to the other and back, is expensive. Then to demand it cheap and make a fuss about it seems strange!

Take bread for instance. The common loaf is so revolting that it has to be recooked by toasting to make it edible and even then it is used only as a vehicle for sticky and greasy substances not otherwise easily consumed. It should be able to stand on its own as a food. We are assured that our wheats are unsuitable for bread making because the product does not keep. Whoever heard of a properly made loaf of fresh bread 'keeping', let alone lasting a meal! Fortunately, since we have joined the Common Market there is some doubt amongst our Continental partners as to whether our bread is a permitted comestible substance at all, doubts at last echoed by the luckless consumers of the substance in their rejection of one of the most loathsome of loaves on offer to the public.

May I offer this threnody?

A GREEN AND PLEASANT LAND

> Weep not, for Wonderloaf is gone.
> I'll put my butter and my jam upon
> A better loaf from a much fairer hand
> 'Tis seen upon the table, now to stand.
> The bakers baked such awful bread
> That mother bakes it now instead.

The future looks good for farmers but certain dangers face this most individualistic body of men. Their very individualism is irksome to many people's thinking; that there should be such a large body of prosperous, independent, out of door fellows, not given to licking anybody's boots (who would on a farm?), is a great stumbling block to those who organise and regiment our lives. Farmers must look to increasing interference in their affairs, especially from the Common Market, that great contriver of bureaucratic confusion. Although it is darkly hinted that the E.E.C. is contrived for the benefit of those French peasants, as yet unpressed into making cars for British motorists, it is a basically benevolent scheme. Its main fault is its complexity, and the beneficiaries are faced with dearer food prices and tales of mountainous surpluses; no amount of explanation will convince people of its virtues and I cannot make it out for myself at times. The danger is that farmers will be blamed for these implausible circumstances.

A surprising inconvenience that farmers face is their excessive wealth. These riches are a paper affluence, only realised if they leave the industry, and many a decent plain farmer finds himself now amongst the latest crop of inflation millionaires. Now you might think this situation very pleasant, but the farmer is mystified. He has passed the milestone and reached the realm of substantial wealth and finds himself, at the same time, prey to heavy taxation demands with no actual cash in his pocket. I will not ask you to pity him, but he does deserve a more sympathetic hearing from the powers that be, especially as he neither asked nor sought to obtain such riches.

All in all, farming sounds too good to be true. I have stressed the variety of interesting work and the pleasant surroundings, but I have been lucky to live in an area where farming is mixed; cattle, sheep, corn, all side by side, with the farmer going from one to the other. There are places and jobs that are not so interesting and readers fresh from rolling in forty acres of grass seeds will want to contradict this happy picture. There are huge dull acreages of corn and potatoes, safely well to the East of where I live and in those places monotony prevails alongside the worst labour relations in the whole industry; so as you eat your food, wholesome or otherwise, home-grown or imported, spare a thought for the farmer who started the whole lengthy process from which you are so safely removed. Remember an American adage I saw recently, 'Don't complain about farmers with your mouth full'.

Four
Bricks and Mortar

All the basic activities of early man have their modern counterpart in a landowner's life and work. I have described the woods which produce firewood, building materials and harbour game; and will mention later the field sports that collect the game and draw off and expend our aggressive natures where required; likewise collecting, a sophisticated activity that reflects our ancestors' preoccupation with food for the winter and has saved many families in the longer winters of economic famine, government or self induced as the case may be. Now I come to building; another basic necessity, that of getting a roof over one's head.

A landowner's life is much given over to this matter. He may or may not be the owner of an enormous house, but he certainly has to attend to many lesser houses and buildings. Much of his time and most of his spare money goes towards an endless round of repairs and improvements.

In the past when a landowner wanted to build, most of his materials and labour came from his estate and cost him very little and this accounts for their excessive preoccupation with grandiose housing. It was then a reasonable hobby; the ruinous expense came in fitting out the enormous shell with fancy goods from outside, fireplaces, hangings and furniture. Nowadays nearly everything is 'imported' from outside the estate and the cost is very great; likewise the labour force wants and deserves a decent wage

THE WORK

to match its skills. Times have changed and the landowner must use great cunning if he is to go on building on any scale at all. I was faced with this problem and shall describe how I set about solving it.

As a family we had always been interested in bricks and mortar; it is a wonderfully durable way of expressing yourself out of doors. My grandmother had inherited the taste from her father who was for ever altering and enlarging his houses. Towards the end of the Victorian era he had built a huge and dressy Queen Anne mansion set in a Sussex parkland; a competent if fulsome work by Sir Reginald Blomfield, who was a sort of Norman Shaw with taste. My grandmother always had some work in hand somewhere in the village; usually it was a cottage being modernised or rebuilt. She employed a small firm of builders in the village whose prosperity was founded on her custom. She built over two dozen houses and cottages and several sets of farm buildings, as well as her own house which was the biggest thing she undertook. Her real success was that she and the builder discovered the correct idiom in which to build a cottage. It is easier to say what it was not, rather than to detail its appearance and appointments. Her cottages were not nineteenth century estate cottages, nor were they twentieth century 'wee nesties', neither did they look like council houses or suburban residences: they were just good, plain homes, built of stone for preference, with steep pitched roofs and plenty of space inside. It sounds easy enough to achieve but in practice it is very rarely done, because the buildings put up today lack balance and balance is what comes when the right materials are used with taste and a sense of proportion by honest craftsmen. When building, endless small sums can be laid out on fripperies; things like barge and facia boards that have to be painted. Good proportions cost nothing, but there must be someone there to indicate them. Her one failing was drains and plumbing; if she could, she left them out, and this is where I came in as I shall recount later.

My father's interest in building was not as strong as his mother's, but it took such a peculiar turn that it bears telling in some detail. He was content to leave unaltered and undecorated the house he was brought up in, but when he did build there were two things uppermost in his mind: concrete and the next world war. Of the first he could never have enough, the second he awaited hourly and was eventually well rewarded in 1939. He had seen and admired the Maginot Line in France, probably doubting its efficacy, but this did not stop him and long before the war broke out he had built half a dozen military affairs of concrete about the village. Three of these were air raid shelters but fortunately the German high command never realised the importance of the village as a tactical target and so their strength was not tried. Two were modest brick and concrete holes dug for his tenantry. The third was a much grander affair in his own grounds, its entrance echoing the front door across the gravel drive. A flight of steps led down into his own underworld; at the bottom was a long brick-lined and vaulted passage that zig-zagged to counter the effect of bomb blast. It ended in another steep tapering staircase that came out just by the edge of the road; from this eyrie the occupant could say nasty things to road users. From here, before a Home Guard exercise, my father captured a demonstration squad of Guardsmen and thereafter declined to join in the proposed exercise on the grounds that he had won already! That was not all; from the main passage two more tunnels ran down deeper and joined up, leading to the living quarters, a concrete and brick room lined with bins like a wine cellar; an iron door gave additional security to these lavish arrangements and as children we much enjoyed the amenities. Now at 10p a time it is opened at garden fêtes as a curiosity. At the top of the garden in the orchard was the strong point, a part-sunk concrete fortlet with deep window embrasures ending in steel plate windows. The internal accommodation was meagre, having only two rooms. After my father's death I went into it for the first time, a belated adventure due to the key being lost for two decades. Elsewhere in the village he built two pigsties with concrete roofs innocently covered with tiles; slots were made in the brickwork from which the Germans could be discomfited as they came over the hills.

My own interest in building was stimulated by two things, the need to modernise the houses my grandmother had owned and a generous and unexpected supply of building materials of the best quality. The job of modernising nearly two dozen substandard cottages seemed too large ever to be started. Employing builders is very expensive, and the modest rents were swallowed by estate duty for the eight years of statutory ruin imposed by a far sighted legislature on those trying to solve the nation's housing problems. At last when these were paid off, there still did not seem to be the money to undertake the work, and I realised I would have to do it myself with such help as I could get. The first house I modernised was a bedroom into bathroom job. A kindly plumber guided my blowtorch and mended the leaks after I had finished. Since then I have had to do a great deal of simple plumbing. It is not the difficult job that people imagine it to be; it could best be described as three dimensional Meccano with a hole down the middle. A few simple rules have to be remembered, likewise the basic layout of pipework; the skills involved are not very great for the type of work I was doing and can be learnt in a day or two. Leaving my first house bubbling with hot water, I went on to do a pair of cottages, converting their useless little front rooms into bathrooms and making the drains, septic tank and soakaways. Here I came to terms with drains; not a subject that raises universal enthusiasm as people are content to ignore what happens underground as long as it does not show itself. Drains have a fascination of their own and would appeal to anybody who has enjoyed damming small streams when a child. 'Downhill all the way' is the golden rule; modern materials have made the work simple, the pipes are made of plastic and just push together. I next graduated to adding extensions to three unmodernised cottages in a row. These were done in stone and I learnt a great deal watching one of my helpers who was good at this type of work. Some of the houses had to have sewage pumps because they had been built in poor sites beside sunken roads and had no drainage; this added much to the expense and complexity of the work and I do not doubt that they will fail on Christmas Eve. Recently all this work has been finished; every house I am responsible for has a lavatory and hot water and I never want to modernise another house in my life. My father used to say he felt like Henry Ford if he made two of anything and I feel the same. I committed some substantial errors, but making them good has been a further education in building. Various fanciful notions and ideas I had on building proved very silly and need not be tried again. One of the greatest benefits was that I became intimately acquainted with all the occupants, who, I hope, found me a human and not just a rapacious rent collector. I was certainly dilatory and slow like all the other builders I have known. One house in particular I remember with the greatest pleasure. In it lived an old retired groom of ninety and his wife who was somewhat younger; constantly people poured in and out of the house, children on the look out for biscuits and never sent empty handed away, relations, friends, delivery men, all were welcome including the landlord. The house seemed to be awash with laughter from dawn till dusk, yet they had nothing much to thank life for: with only the bare minimum of a pension, looking after the very old when you yourself are fairly old cannot be easy.

As a sort of builder and bodger I was very lucky to have an unusual education in the trade. This was the demolition of a large country house just outside the village. I entered into the work with enthusiasm and greatly enjoyed myself, more, I must hasten to add, because of the acquisitions I made rather than the sheer love of destruction. Since that time a strong movement has grown up to preserve all such places, and this movement has an indiscriminate wish to rescue all houses rather than concentrate on those deserving preservation, so I fear its energies may be dissipated. This house was devoid of any merit and I had no qualms in helping destroy it. It was a large Victorian house built in the manner loosely described as Georgian, i.e. it had sash windows and trimmings in the classical taste. It had been built in the 1850's by a local landowner. He had overreached himself in building it and his descendants disposed of the property in the 1890's to a rich family from the north of England who further enlarged and embellished the house, only to fade away during the first World War and be replaced by a Scottish family. The last inhabitant had been a charming but wayward dowager, devoted to animal welfare, who had died in 1952 and since then the house had stood shuttered and empty, the property of a charity devoted to the last occupant's good causes.

BRICKS AND MORTAR

When I heard that it was to be demolished I went to the house and met a stocky, rough looking man with one eye and a squint in what was left of his sight: he was in that high good humour that such contractors always have when they are taking on a lorry load of lead a day. Everything was for sale on the condition that you removed it as soon as possible. 'Do you want that room of panelling? Yours for £100'. 'Will nobody buy these marble pillars? I'll help you get them down'. 'There is a nice fireplace out the back. I'll give it to you for £20'. I succumbed to the many temptations and spent money I had not got, nor have I regretted it.

Inside the house, chaos reigned. The windows had been taken out to obtain the lead sash weights, likewise the missing lead on the roof let in steady streams of water. Undistributed pamphlets on animal welfare spiralled and fluttered in the grand marbled hall like a flock of tumbler pigeons. Huge placards urged you to save the pit ponies from the mine, coal mines that were a great source of income to the last occupants. Underwear of a voluminous and antique cut was draped about at the whim of the house-breaker's humour, for the house had been sold with all its contents. All the while men were throwing cast-iron radiators out of the upstairs windows.

I bought slates and timber, stone, fireplaces, floors, windows and finally three hundred lorryloads of rubble for farm roads, all in one long indiscriminate spending spree. I worked so hard that my back wore out and I dreamed at night of being crushed by falling masonry. Amongst my more ludicrous purchases was the front porch, a heavy classical arrangement of pillars round a triumphal arch; this I secured for £25 and as it proved to be held together with copper bars, I even made a profit. Less wisely I bought the marble pillars in the hall and removed them without breakage, leaving everything they supported intact if dangerous; a feat of ingenuity I shall not attempt to repeat. They lie to this day, an unwanted and immovable nuisance in a barn. As the house was stripped, I saw the whole business of high quality building revealed without having to attend on the slow process of doing it. It was a sort of potted course in construction studied in reverse, and at the end of it all I had the materials to do it again the right way round, on a smaller scale.

My first building to be planned and made from the great regular slabs of ashlar masonry rescued from the demolition was a stable. My house had been built since the introduction of motor cars and so was unprovided in this respect. Formerly my horses had lived in some tumbledown buildings in the village, now nothing would be too good for them. On the strength of my building materials I became converted to neo-palladianism, an architectural creed that many would consider out-dated and unsuitable for a stable. I had always been much impressed by those eighteenth century palaces of the horse attached to country houses and determined to have one for myself, although on a reduced scale. The plan was a simple rectangular block with a central doorway, the horses turning left and right into their looseboxes as they entered; a space in between served as a store for food and harness. My neo-palladianism was concentrated on the front, where I pulled forward by six inches the central third of the facade containing the double doors of the entrance and capped it with a pediment. The piece of wall either side contained a tall arched window entirely filled with random rubble as a contrast to the fine cut stonework elsewhere; the pediment was treated in the same way. This facade was carried up above the eaves as a parapet with a lead-lined gutter behind that has leaked ever since. The roof is of Cornish slates in graduated courses, small at the top and large at the bottom, and the ridge was dressed in lead. A ventilator stands in the centre of the roof and reflects the design of the pediment in front and leaks as well.

The finished impression is formal and precise. It is out of keeping with the other buildings nearby made of rougher stone with steep tiled roofs. The blind windows either side of the door aroused fierce controversy amongst neighbouring architectural critics; some disapproved as they served no purpose, others wanted the horses to look out of them, but I will state it a firm rule of stable building that if a horse can look out it will get out, usually by kicking and pushing the door down. The two real windows were at the back and I made a mistake by selecting the worst possible position for them, placing them on the plain blank wall so that the distance between them equalled their distance from the ends of the building. I have since planted pear trees on this wall to fuzz over this error. My other mistake was that I was not technically competent to carry out the lead work, which has leaked and blown up in gales or filled with beech mast ever since, and I would avoid building parapet walls in front of roofs if doing the job again. As a stable it has been a great success, and this success was mainly due to the two excellent stonemasons employed and a simple layout. I was only responsible for the roofs and woodwork throughout the building.

The next scheme for my amusement was the reconstruction of the front porch that I had bought from the demolition for £25. Originally it had sheltered people alighting at the front door from carriages: I decided to reassemble it in a clump of trees half a mile away from my house in the valley that I describe elsewhere. Having no lifting cranes or dismantling machinery, I laid a bed of bales round the building and threw off the heavy cornice; this proved so heavy that I could not do much with it and I sold it to a monumental mason. That left me with the pillars and these I pulled down like rotten trees onto the bales below with very little damage. The concrete raft that formed the ceiling of the porch was first jacked up with a hydraulic lorry jack with a long pine pole on top of it. Once the weight was off the pillars they wobbled about easily, and on the ground they could be rolled about like huge cheeses. Each section was a different size and had to be marked for eventual rebuilding.

The plan of the temple I proposed was simple. It was four pillars wide and two pillars deep; between the two centre pillars at the back was a seat and a curtain wall, the floor area was about 18 feet by 9 feet. First I dug seven holes and filled them with concrete; over two of these I erected a wobbly framework of scaffolding from which I hung a chain pulley on a ring that could slide to and fro on a scaffolding pole. The cheese-like sections of the pillars had fan-shaped slots in their top surfaces; into these a set of 3 wedges were inserted and pinned together so they could not come out. They were then hooked on and raised by the pulley to the right height, slid sideways on the ring and bar and dropped with a plop onto the mortar. The work was very simple, so simple that the stature of the builders of the Parthenon diminished in my eyes. By good luck or the law of averages the tops of the capitals were all level within half an inch. Having sold the original cornice, I had to make a concrete one; to do this I made a wooden box along the tops of the pillars and filled it with concrete and empty wine bottles to eke out my mix. Unfortunately I under-estimated the weight of liquid concrete and my wood-work bellied and distorted under pressure. This later had to be rectified by plastering over the more obvious defects. A more experienced person would have cast mouldings on the front of the lintel, but this was beyond my capacity and I have had to settle for a more rustic interpretation of a classical temple. I did recreate the dentelles, large square protrusions associated with classical mouldings, and this came about by laying eight large oak timbers across the building from front to back, protruding a foot or more. On this raft I built the roof but I had to contrive bogus beam-ends on the sides by bolting pieces of the same timber to the two outermost beams. I could not land the rafters of the roof on these short pieces as the weight would have pushed them down and out, so the rafters land on a purlin inside the roof and the bottom two foot length of each rafter rests on nothing. Rafter bottoms always rot so there is one less maintenance job. Dentelles in classical mouldings are said to represent beam ends, so I was glad that they reappeared of their own accord as a working part of the building. The roof is made of clay pantiles. Roman tiles would have been more authentic but the effect is similar. The gable end of the roof forms a classical pediment and is made of wood, the exposed bits being covered with lead. Later I cut a round hole in the middle.

Some people would reckon that there were more important things to do in life than build classical follies and I can assure them it was a Sunday and spare time job, spread over three years or more: building something very useful in a nasty place like the edge of a town is praiseworthy but not nearly so interesting as building something beautiful on an outstanding site; this is a real treat and an opportunity not to be missed.

THE WORK

I have other schemes afoot and have mentioned elsewhere my ambitions for a pagoda. This will never come about because of the detailed brickwork which is beyond my skills, and I plan to use the site for a small castle-like tower with a large arch to one side. I long wanted a Palladian-style room attached to one end of my house but this has been vetoed by the person responsible for the inside of the house on the grounds that it is unnecessary and would collect dust. Far more useful would be the almshouses that my grandmother planned before the last war but never built. It would not do nowadays to call them almshouses, but the need for such things is as large as ever, especially in small villages where the stock of housing is limited and constantly taken up by weekenders. Small purpose-built houses of this type enable old people to stay in their community (that is, if it is a real community with helpers around) for years more than they can survive in other places where they are taken off to a thinly disguised workhouse on the first onset of real old age. From the builders' point of view such a plan has a lot to recommend it; planning permission would be easily granted and two such houses could be built for the price of one normal sized house. Furthermore, two full sized houses would be released for larger families when the new occupants moved in. It is not generally realised that there is no house shortage in this country; the trouble is house usage, shown by countless empty bedrooms.

As a pastime building has much to recommend it: it is like a huge jigsaw that you go on adding bits to interminably. It involves many different skills so that a versatile person need never be bored by repetition; the physical effort is very good for you. It is strenuous but never uncomfortable; one person can do a tremendous amount by steady application over a long period of time. If I were a medical man I would prescribe it as a hobby preferable to press-ups and squash. Games and suchlike leave behind only a feeling of temporary wellbeing and nothing else. The amateur builder leaves a great deal behind to show for his exercise although it is sometimes in doubtful taste.

Five
An Old Saw

To be a carpenter is a humble vocation, yet God selected a carpenter's household for his own Son and this has been a great consolation to the trade ever since, who, when twitted on some imagined shortcoming of their profession, can refer to this divine favour as no small recompense. Nowadays you rarely meet such a thing as a carpenter plain and simple as the trade has divided itself into many divisions. You meet joiners and cabinet makers, shipwrights and wheelwrights, roofing contractors and floorlayers, but only rarely a carpenter. If I am to have a trade, this is mine and I have dabbled in all the crafts just mentioned with the exception of shipwright, not reaching great proficiency in any one field but saving myself a great deal of money through not having to employ somebody else. When the red revolution comes I shall stand up and be counted a carpenter. Luckily totalitarian regimes always lead to such a marked decay in standards that my shortcomings as a woodworker will be overlooked.

I did not become a carpenter by preference or apprenticeship; I became one by inheritance. This claim might be considered ludicrous because you are not supposed to inherit skills or even predispositions towards some craft or work. Statistical evidence to back up the possibility of my claim is not available because carpenters rarely keep long records going back a couple of centuries, which is about as

AN OLD SAW

long as an inherited trait can be recognised. Your joiner met in the street will be able to tell you what his father and grandfather did, but before that you will draw blank. It is only among those people who have made good that such information is preserved, and that is the last place a researcher would look. Quite understandably he does not expect to find or look for evidence of the heritability of skills amongst the rich, but it is just such a place that he should look because they have kept the 'ancestral memory'; by this I mean that they know what their forbears were doing two hundred years ago because they did it so well that written records are left behind of their prowess.

Among my own ancestors there was a clique of carpenters. In the late eighteenth century a group of boat building families lived, worked and intermarried at Rochester on the mouth of the Medway, generating, I believe, a powerful disposition towards woodworking. One of these families left shipbuilding for banking and prospered in the way described so well in Galsworthy's novels; amongst them was my great grandfather who was particularly successful as a banker, but underneath, all the time, lurked the carpenter. In his spare time he would make model boats; not little cotton rigged dust-catchers, but simple half ship forms of mahogany such as boat builders still make. His carpentry found another outlet; denied by convention the pleasures of altering his houses himself, he constantly had builders about the place, enlarging and altering his homes; recreating the bustle of the shipyard. So strong was the trait that even his eldest daughter, whom I can only just remember as a very old spinster given over to good works, had a small workshop in the cellars. Naturally my father also had a workshop in which he spent a lot of time. He was a metal worker rather than a carpenter and was prepared

THE WORK

to make anything. He was the only man I ever heard of who made his own collar studs of turned brass, deeming the commercial article inferior. His talents were mainly devoted to gunmaking and repairing his collections, but when he did make or repair domestic articles they re-entered home life solid and utterly indestructible. His workshop was very untidy, he could never find any tools he wanted and at the same time poured scorn on tidiness as a virtue in such places. Small, easily lost tools, such as centre punches, he would buy in half dozens and broadcast down the length of the workshop from the door. Here he was happy, he could scream and shout, as was his wont, to relieve his feelings. He hated to be disturbed, and on approaching the workshop I would break into a tuneless whistle and so spare myself the anger and simulated shock that he put on for any unexpected intruder. Once inside I was quite welcome and was allowed to do jobs beside him. It was here I learnt two excellent lessons – if you want something, make it, and never be frightened to have a go, however improbable the undertaking.

My own career as a carpenter started at school at the age of eight or nine, where this useful subject appeared on the curriculum. I was much taken by the work and wished to practise at home, so one Christmas a carpenter's bench and tools were given to me. Alas, no wood was included in the gift. I rushed to the gardener's shed and found a packing case, dismembered it and remade it as a disgusting bookcase and eventually retired from the workshop very disgruntled. Years elapsed before I took to working with my hands again; constructive or mechanical ingenuity eluded me. I was the boy who couldn't mend a puncture, pick a padlock or even tie a bowline on the bite. How I envied others who did all these things and made crystal sets

AN OLD SAW

too. Now the tables are turned. The ingenious companions of my youth are locked in some tedious occupation that has no call for these talents. I look down with contempt on those poor mortals who solve all their problems by sending for a man; how can they resist the challenge of having a go at it themselves? In my late 20's I became for a short while a jobbing carpenter. How I hated people who 'sent for a man'; demanding the quality of Chippendale for the price of a cheap jack, yet this abrasive nitpicking is the source of all quality and finish. For nine months I worked doing odd jobs in wood and had I continued for nine years I might have become a good carpenter. Changing circumstances caused me to give up this type of work and I became a general builder, modernising and mending the houses for which I was responsible. I became plumber and tiler, stonemason and glazier; all trades that are interesting but best jumbled up with each other for variety's sake. To do any one all the time would be less amusing. Jack of all trades, master of none, is how the saying goes and I am one; despised by the steady slow-moving craftsmen but very useful, as anyone knows who has had a plumber in the house who will not carpenter, or vice versa. Your craftsman has to send out for another and so the expense is greatly increased. These rigid craft divisions are made by people who are overproud of having a few simple skills. My work does not allow the time to pander to these susceptibilities; it is a running battle with rotting wood, porous stone and leaking pipes, all to be paid out of controlled rents; a strong job is all I can aspire to.

What are the pleasures of carpentry? You may laugh when I say that there is a positive physical pleasure to be derived from the sensation of steel cutting wood, it is akin to smelling or tasting. I cannot offer any reason why this should be so; suffice that it is there and might as well be enjoyed since it is both innocent and useful. Some tools are a greater pleasure to use than others; the common handsaw is bracing rather than anything else more subtle; the plane is an improvement and the chisel one of the pleasantest: to hammer a chisel straight across the grain of wood is unrewarding, but when the edge goes surely along with the grain it is a pleasant thing. The drawknife, a rarer tool usually used by wheelwrights, is even more pleasant to work with; it is a fair return for the dreadful tribulation of making a wooden wheel. The cabinet maker has little call for it except when chamfering church pews or making a cabriole leg. This latter, much used on eighteenth century chairs and tables, is one of the finest expressions of a wood worker's art. At last he is freed from the discipline of the straight and regular; only the eye can compare and measure. One cabriole leg is easy but not very useful except when repairing, two on a chair have to match each other; you can measure the length but otherwise they are too formless for a rule to be much use, yet when assembled any error in matching is noticeable, even to the untutored eye.

The ordinary carpenter does not need a huge number of tools before he sets to work, and many years can be spent exploring their possibilities. I tend to eschew gadgets with the exception of a mechanical sander and saw, for a run of sawing is good exercise and gives you time to reconsider the work in hand. I do not even despise old tools and once, when my market town failed to produce a one inch morticeing chisel I found a blacksmith-made one in an antique shop which I was able to put to good use. The choice of woods is usually very narrow and I am perplexed that carpenters should not be more adventurous in this respect. For making a small piece of furniture you do not

AN OLD SAW

need a vast amount of wood and even a fallen branch can be milled up at less cost than common deals bought. Mulberry trees yield a magnificent honey coloured timber with an interesting grain and the colour of the best Queen Anne walnut, although please do not cut down a tree for this purpose alone. The acacia tree, so widely promoted by William Cobbett, gives a hard yellow wood, harder and more durable than oak. Unfortunately it grows so twisted and wrinkled that it is disliked by sawyers on account of the wastage; if it has a future it will be used like sweet chestnut and grown for fence posts from coppiced stools. It grows very quickly, a seed sown in the year of the great drought of 1976 grew 42 inches in four months; any tree to do that deserves more than cursory attention. Hawthorn was used by French ebenistes in the eighteenth century and has an unusual pinkish tint. Fruitwoods are also rewarding timbers to work with, especially pearwood but the woodworms are very partial to it. It is a sad state of affairs that the finest timber trees like walnut fetch huge prices, only to be converted into flashy bedroom suites in a debased style that is a negation of all that honest carpentry stands for.

The great problem is what to make. I have been overrun by necessity and spent too much time with rough sawn 2 ins. x 4 ins. timber doing dull repairs. The amateur has more leisure to look about and choose some suitable thing on which to exercise his skills: he should avoid the textbooks as these show only the most horrible designs. Far better to spend time looking at good furniture, ancient and modern, in museums and exhibitions and then decide, having photographs and sketches to hand. A chair is always a good test of skill, as the joints are subject to great strain. If your first chair falls to pieces in use, it is a noble end and you can always make another, stronger. Wood carving is a happy backwater, devouring endless time and great skill. The trouble is that there is little call for carved work these days; for ease of construction furniture is blessedly free from it. The tour de force of carving, say a trophy of game, is useless by itself. It lies around gathering dust and causing anxiety to its proud perpetrator lest the snipe's beak gets broken; hung on the wall they look like a brown mess, however clever the work and deep the undercutting. To apply carving to furniture is very wrong as the world is already full of grotesque chairs, a riot of misplaced chisel work. The carver's skills so often run ahead of his taste and discretion: possibly the newel posts of staircases are the only places to carry such work satisfactorily, but then it is usually a muddle of bogus armorials swathed in dragons or some such conceit, and who, anyway, these days, has newel posts? It is a pity this labour can find no worthwhile outlet, so let the woodcarver turn sculptor and exchange trade for the arts. The best furniture is simple and well proportioned; the ambitious carpenter, his bandsaw already singing, longs to cast off the shackles of good plain line and weave fancy free through the wood on impulse alone: it would be better if he made jigsaws. In Victorian times the introduction of bandsaws and other machines freed the cabinet maker from the discipline of straight wood grain; the results were often regrettable. The secret is not to avoid curves but to control them within the thickness of the wood and its grain, for if you fret a bit of wood out like Harry Lauder's walking stick it will assuredly break, as no piece of wood except that one famous exception is grown that way. The discipline needed to make something plain and decent is far greater than the skills required to spoil work with meretricious ornament.

What, you will ask no doubt, has your stern lecturer on

purity of line and woodgrain made? The answer is a bit of everything; discounting plain structural work such as roofs, doors and floors, I have repaired all manner of furniture and now would not give a Regency sabre legged chair houseroom for fear of the inevitable work needed to keep its legs together. I regret not having made more furniture and what I have done lacks finish. The designs are acceptable but the tedious sanding is not done as well as it ought to be. In the hurry to get onto the next job, this finishing is skimped as it takes as much time as the rest of the work and is not so interesting as the actual fabrication of a piece of furniture. Amongst other things that I have been tempted or forced to make are cupboards, bookcases, kitchen units, cannon carriages, a pony carriage (rebuilt), gunstocks, a barn (which leaks due to an error of my helper), a sofa (comfortable), lorry bodies (3), staircases (5), picture frames (hopeless failures), greenhouse cum conservatory, field gates, a candlestick, a jardiniere, windows, doorknobs, curtain pulls, tables, stools, and once I tried to make a wheel but that was also an utter failure. On another occasion I missed the opportunity of remaking my cousin's wooden leg and was denied a unique addition to my catalogue, a catalogue that shows the wide variety of jobs that can be undertaken if you are prepared to have a go. Very rarely have I got to professional standards, but likewise I doubt if a professional would try to make such a range of artifacts or ever be offered the variety.

Having so many other things to do diminishes considerably the time I have for carpentry and some schemes are a long time unfinished; the blacksmith and I had a cannon carriage under construction for twelve years until finally we made a day of it, hammering and chiselling side by side. In a corner of my workshop the blacksmith and I have started the ultimate in schemes, a monocycle following a seventeenth century Italian design. So far we have only made a spokeless wheel six foot high. Within this circuit it is intended that a bicycle-like frame on small wheels should run, riding up the inner circumference and so propelling the whole ludicrous contrivance along. The motive power is by handles and ropes and the courageous rider is to sit within. The monocycle in this form preceded our bicycle and judging by the sturdy scale of this particular specimen, it will be with us long after the last bicycle has rusted away from the face of the earth: all in all a wonderfully silly notion and therein lies its appeal.

A man's workshop is now his castle. No longer can the home aspire to this grandiose title; he is for much of the year only a nocturnal visitor, yet here I am, recommending that he should shut himself up even in his spare time at weekends, away from his family and engrossed in an occupation whose results may not be necessary or useful to his family. It is a sad defect of our times that so many people are tied to occupations well outside their natural inclination. It would be wise to pander to any urge to make things, ghastly and useless though they may be. A man whose life is devoted to applying plastic trim to the insides of cheap saloon cars must occasionally yearn to do things worthwhile. The workshop, maybe only a corner of the garage, is the scene of these necessary ambitions, even if they rise no higher than the manufacture of marquetry tea trays or elephant-shaped book ends.

Although not bound by working hours or a dull job, I too rush to the workshop if time allows, with the enthusiasm of a sweaty person about to swim on a hot day. Time flies by, the preoccupation and concentration is enormous,

AN OLD SAW

meals cool unnoticed, interruptions are terribly received and I am as happy as can be. How much more will a person tied to an uncongenial job yearn to do likewise.

THE DIVERSIONS

Six
Household Gods

Collecting works of art may not seem a very important part of a landowner's life; many will declare that they are too busy or too poor to think of such a thing, forgetting that in many cases they are still in business only because some forbear collected works of art. A good mixed country house collection is part of the collateral finance of an estate. The expression 'collateral finance' is quite as ugly as it sounds and it means all the investments a landowner has outside his property. The more collateral money he has, the more pleasant life is for everybody on his estate.

His collections of pictures, furniture, etc. are not unlike a country's gold reserves; distant, untouchable and little use in themselves. It behoves him to treat them with respect and not dispose of them lightly. They are the things he was brought up with and may well be fond of; nobody wants an empty space over the fireplace where a family portrait was once hung. Stocks and shares, another form of collateral finance, are dull things and in theory can be repurchased, though they rarely are. Ancestors, on the other hand, are the very devil to buy back!

On this collateral money a landowner can borrow, raise large sums of capital by sale if he must, or use it as a set dressing for a tourist attraction. Rarely, nowadays, does he think to replenish or augment his collections. All this century an attitude of lusty philistinism has been the order of the day in the country houses of England. I cannot give any advice on so complicated a subject as forming a collection, but the notes that follow give some idea of how collections have come about.

Man is an acquisitive brute; he naturally hoards things against hard times. Many of us save money if we can but it is a dull, convertible asset about which you are supposed neither to talk nor boast. There are people who, given sufficient for their daily needs, prefer to put their surplus into goods; some, from a warranted distrust of paper money, keep gold bars; the more adventurous derive pleasure from risking their cash by collecting things; as a sort of human they are fascinating and sometimes unpleasant. It is worth while to look at such people, to enquire into their habits and motives. I do not refer to those who have inherited fine collections but to the actual makers of the collection. I am the fourth generation of my family to be a confirmed hoarder and putter by, so I have seen and can even now feel the mechanism at work.

A collector's motives are not always very estimable. I am sure a psychologist would find much to despise in them. At one end of the range is the pub crawler slipping beer mats into his pocket; at the other, people like Lord Hertford and William Beckford. The two extremities rarely meet, which is not a bad thing for both parties and it enables me to divide collectors into two sorts.

The humbler, more numerous and amiable portion are that vast regiment of bottlers, match boxers, beer matters and philatelists. The latter will be annoyed to be so relegated and I can almost hear the angry closing of albums as they set out to do battle, pincers aloft; but there they are, relegated because their work, like that of the others, is making a series, compiling a set of something: like bees in the hive, every cell must be filled with honey and they labour indefatigably to this end. They share many of the pleasures of collecting like finding the bargain, the excitement of the chase or even gloating over the value of their accumulations. The instinct is close to that of squirrels, it is as primaeval as getting in the harvest or making a fine heap of firewood to last the whole winter. Our advanced and effete society denies to most people these simpler forms of collecting; bread is bought at the bakery rather than made from corn taken from a granary, coal is delivered by the ton, noisily and suddenly. So it is no surprise that the thrifty squirrel-like urge, when still with us, is played out on some small, eminently collectable, easily containable substitute. But here is the sadness, such hoards are born only to die; the granary is emptied, the wood pile dwindles, each incursion into the stocks is accompanied by a self-congratulatory paean in praise of one's thrift and foresight. This pleasure is not available to the latter day descendants of the farmers and woodcutters putting by their winter stores and so it is that our modern collector, having completed his series, finished the set, made up the run or just 'got them all' is bored and disillusioned. Fortunately for their sakes this does not come about easily, the most affected are the intense specialists, the 'Gossware only' man: the 'got all the pennies' (except 1933) man. I know of a man who collected Baxter prints, a charming little Victorian backwater. His affluence and determination acquired for him a specimen of every one and immediately on completion, the whole collection was despatched to the auction rooms. The philatelist can usually emigrate, likewise the coin collector can go classical, but the specialist is doomed unless he broadens his outlook. Another thing these collections share with their primeval ancestors is dullness. Stores of corn and heaps of

THE DIVERSIONS

wood may be satisfying but are visually dull; likewise one Toby jug is amusing, two is a brace and ten are a bore. To remedy this defect the more sensitive collector resorts to making patterns; at one end of the scale the beer mats are pinned with skill and care to the bedroom wall in the students' digs, at the other end the gold étuis and bonbonnières lie cosseted on velvet in subtly lit vitrines. The effect is the same, only the price is different.

Leaving the squirrels behind we come to the more interesting sort of collector; more interesting because they dig deeper into their pockets, the objects they collect are more attractive and the motives more varied and often downright nasty. No collector except the very simplest fits into one type neatly; the motives are confused and many. A man can collect renaissance bronzes with the mentality of a beer matter and presumably vice versa, though Heaven forbid that I should meet either of them.

Firstly there are the escapists, if I may call them such because they are escaping from the realities of life. Usually it starts as a harmless piece of romanticism and gets no further. He or she, inspired by the suavely drawn cover of a novel by Georgette Heyer and later perusal of the contents, decides life would have been more pleasant in those distant times; they set about creating that world in their own home and this they do by collecting furniture, pictures and objects made in the period they admire. The creation of this ambience gives them endless pleasure and some profit if they have bought wisely. In France it assumes the proportions of a national industry; modern furniture design stagnates, life is hardly supportable unless lived in a watered down miniature Versailles. Luckily for us in England civilization lingered on after the 1790's and quite bearable epochs of taste date from after this time and have been considered well worth recreating. Recently I was in a successful copy of a late Victorian gentleman's snuggery, the type of room in which John Buchan's raconteurs tell their stories. No doubt in the north of Scotland, dusty and unchanged, the genuine article lingers on. The vanity of it turns to vice when the resident escapist starts to dress the part, usually donning a voluminous cloak; at that juncture we can leave him as he becomes more than faintly ridiculous and pass on to the other sort of fugitive.

The saddest sort of collector is he who has turned from his fellow men in disgust and transferred his affections, such as remain, to inanimate objects. They indubitably make the greatest collections of all and it would seem that the greater the collection, the nastier the man who made it. Names such as William Beckford, Sir Richard Wallace and Sir Thomas Philips come to mind. William Beckford inherited an enormous fortune, was ostracized for a then unfashionable and heinous crime; he then turned to his collections and architectural fantasies for comfort, locked in his embattled palaces, surrounded by obsequious servants, his scouts rootling across whole continents bringing home only the very best. This type of collector avoids the rough and tumble of the auction rooms and shops, which is wise as his very presence inflates the prices. An unattractive element of gloating possessiveness develops; this is the result of the collectors' antisocial habits, they become suspicious and secretive about their treasures. As they grow older they forget how much they have, lose things and accuse relations of taking them.

We cannot all be Beckfords so we must reconcile ourselves to follow a more moderate course in our collections. Excepting those who make specialised collections, it is reasonable to surround ourselves with as many decent things as we can procure and then live with them. My own collecting goes no further than wanting to live amongst a decent cross section of artistic endeavour, past and present; in no way an objectionable ambition. I have seen too much of the vices of collecting and am anxious to avoid them. Note that I say 'procure and live with' for once it becomes difficult to live with your collection, you have gone too far.

I was brought up in a sort of private Victoria and Albert museum founded by my great grandfather, a rich Victorian banker of Quaker stock, cast in a Galsworthian mould of thrift, integrity and toil. To be a Quaker and interested in the visual arts is unusual as members of this society tended to eschew such worldly matters. Learned papers have been written on the high incidence of colour blindness amongst them and this must atrophy their artistic sensibilities. My great grandfather's first love was Chinese blue and white porcelain which enjoyed a vogue then and now. From this he moved to other types of oriental china, keeping wisely to Chinese china for Chinamen, always avoiding export wares and the huge flashy aberrations of taste like famille rose vases 6 feet high, favoured by many English collectors at that time; he even bought contemporary Japanese earthenware, an advanced taste. He left behind meticulous accounts of his collection, making little sketches on the invoices; the objects were labelled also with the source, date of purchase and price in code as well. At the same time he collected pictures, mainly Dutch Old Masters and also paintings by Whistler, dodging the horrors of Alma Tadema and yet never in 30 years falling out with Whistler; no mean achievement. Likewise he collected English eighteenth century furniture, embroideries, drawings and renaissance art in various forms. The most remarkable thing about him was his faultless taste, whatever taste is; yet at the same time he avoided 'ghastly good taste' as well as any of the unpleasant characteristics I have described to which collectors can succumb. He was generous and modest, deferring to the opinions of the most uninformed of people. He died in 1916, leaving behind two large houses filled to the brim with good things and many children, mainly daughters, who by the time they died had disposed of the bulk of the collections by gift and sale. I am, of course, embittered as very little came my way and this is the horrid greed of the collector breaking through my civilized facade. I am also piqued because neither I nor my father were considered suitable custodians. However all was not lost because my grandmother carefully bagged any unwanted items and in this way managed to rescue a number of lovely things that her sisters had no use for. These sisters enjoyed the cachet attached to owning a famous collection rather than enjoying the collection itself. Their lives were packed with good and charitable acts, they helped people in all walks of life, they were good Christians but indifferent heirs to a fine collection. They lived a life of exacting penury surrounded by Rembrandt and Franz Hals paintings: it seemed as if they tried to live not by their income but the annual interest on that income and they nearly succeeded. I once ate cold potato cakes in their company.

As I mentioned, no unconsidered trifle was missed by my grandmother and her wish to collect was satisfied by recollecting family possessions. She did maintain her father's tradition of helping artists, one of them extensively, though his reputation has never 'matured'. I do not doubt his ability but I fear she bought all his best pictures so he has never become famous through that posthumous trading and reappraisal that can sanctify an artist. Her particular protégé meddled in Chinese politics (he was Chinese), disappeared and I cannot say for certain if he is dead.

My father was an only child; his father, a costive naval commander, died young leaving my grandmother to enjoy a widowhood of nearly 60 years during which time she doted on and ignored her son alternately, giving him that ample distrust of human nature which enabled him to turn easily from people to things in later life. He should have been a soldier but an early experiment with explosives cost him an eye; thereafter he was a soldier manqué and travelled widely in Europe and the Middle East for some unspecified branch of the intelligence services. His main interest was guns; these he started collecting more as mechanical curiosities than works of art. Later his tastes developed to cover all weapons from flint arrow-heads to court swords. Collecting weapons often attracts a childish type of person: the would-be cowboy, or gangster, and in my father's case, the might have been soldier. His sense of humour was robust and childish at times, he liked explosions and often made them at the top of the garden. His interests in collecting were several; he liked things for themselves – how they were made, when and where; strange cultural influences and muddles fascinated him; he admired good workmanship, but tempered it with taste and so avoided those terrible 'tours de force' of workmanship that appear in most respectable collections.

As he grew older his interests grew beyond weaponry to include clocks, scientific instruments, oriental art and the books to cover his many interests. His excellent memory and command of several languages enabled him to read much more widely than most scholars and he achieved a manner that was, if not scholarly, convincing and well informed. His good eye and judicious buying were rewarded and he made a fine collection of Tibetan art before such things became fashionable; likewise Persian art, avoiding all the vulgar and tawdry goods that were enthusiastically collected by Persians before their recent revolution.

He was not a sociable man and kept little company except his dealers and two or three friends. Like others before him, he turned from people to things and was genuinely terrified of any emotional involvement or disturbance. In some of his remoter subjects he cannot have met any fellow collectors or authorities, nor could he have ever discussed his current enthusiasms, and this highlights the great loneliness of many collectors' lives; they are suspicious, a visitor might steal, or worse make an offer or talk in a pub about what he had seen. Various visitors did all these things to him at times and his suspicions in old age included his family. This was not pleasant as I was considered an offender in this respect and once received a perfunctory note from him requesting the return of a whole list of things, some valueless trifles that anybody might borrow from their father, while others were things of value he had mislaid. Our relationship cooled somewhat and I saw less of him in his declining years.

After his death it was revealed that he did not deem me a suitable recipient of his hoardings. At first I was upset, more by a trick in which he made me believe I had some expectations in this direction than by the loss of my imagined share. I had appointed myself a sort of honorary curator and was the only person who knew the extent of his collection or even what many of the things were and naturally I had looked forward to enjoying my portion. The real surprise was that I hardly minded this loss despite being filled with a healthy lust for collecting. This was the second time a collection had passed tantalisingly close to my nose but I was cured. After he died the enormous collections and mountains of knowledge seemed vain achievements; the knowledge vanished leaving behind the lumber, soulless without its master.

Seven
Adding to the Hoard

As you already know, I was trained up from an early age to be a collector. When six or thereabouts a large cabin trunk arrived at home; it was once the property of an old sea captain and it was full of curiosities. Tiger's whiskers mounted on a piece of cardboard, the shell of a tortoise, samples of crude rubber from the Brazilian rubber boom, neatly labelled as to their place of origin, fossils, polished geological specimens, even a tuft of hair from a grizzly bear and the quill of a porcupine. I called it my museum. A kind aunt gave me a strange little showcase of mahogany made like a miniature greenhouse. Within I arranged my treasures. My grandmother gave me three tiles taken by herself from the palaces of Pekin, conjuring in my mind the strange picture of this artistically sensitive woman vandalising one of the more accessible eaves of the palaces with her umbrella handle. She also gave me a snuff box made of a cowrie shell bound in silver and an ammonite halved and polished. These and other things I still have and I have resisted the temptation to scatter them in various cabinets; the mahogany greenhouse was neither convenient or attractive and so they all live in a scruffy cardboard box in a cupboard. I still add extraneous items to the hoard; a wooden image of the Holy Nil, an obscure Russian saint; a huge silver gilt mounted meerschaum pipe, some burgomeister's pride and delight; a walnut whelk shell, marvellously smooth, and a mother o' pearl box containing a necklace of lapis lazuli beads from Ur of the Chaldees. About once a year they all come out for a breath of fresh air. Each ridiculous bit reminds me of some remote corner of the world or the moment of childish joy when I first owned it: no one thing is related to any other except in their profound irrelevance to each other and this they share in the decent obscurity of the cardboard box.

When I grew up I decided to collect pictures; I was drawn to a field of collecting unexplored by my father, who was reluctant to pay more than £25 for a picture. He had, of course, bought many pictures but he had bought haphazardly, favouring works illustrative of his other interests. My ambitions went much higher: I wanted art with a capital A, not decorator's pictures, not bad scribbles by great artists to have a good name on my walls, but real paintings by original artists of merit. This all sounds lofty stuff but I do not think it was unreasonable; my idea was to continue the line of collecting that my family had already made. Their taste was typically represented by the paintings of four artists, William Nicholson, Philip Connard, Eve Kirk and James McBey. The first two represented the modern tastes of my great grandfather; the second two, the tastes of my parents when they were first married in the 1930's. It was a very catholic choice; these painters ask no portentous questions, expose no new social issues and puzzle nobody. In short, they are simple paintings done with skill and a great pleasure to live with. In this last clause is to be found the real reason for buying pictures. It may seem tame, but who wants a gaudy exposition of some social injustice on their walls; nor did I want advanced and theoretical paintings. The vogue for such paintings seems on the wane now and to own a picture of a recognisable subject is no longer a crime.

My ambitions to own a landscape by William Nicholson were thwarted by rising prices that marched ahead of my purse all the time, and still do. He is the only one of my four artists who is generally known; his son is passing famous for a sort of picture beyond my ken. In the meantime I have to be satisfied with a family portrait that I borrowed from a great-aunt who sat for it in the early years of the century, just before he wearied at the popular demand for his portraits. She sits on a table top that comprises the foreground, dressed for riding and in much the same position, her gloves, crop and a flower forming a typical Nicholson still life on the table top; the remaining three quarters of the picture shows a huge dull brown canvas with the rudimentary outlines of a ramping horse and rider drawn in. It is a picture of a picture with the sitter by accident in the bottom right hand corner. This may sound complicated, but it enabled the artist to paint a rather pert little madam and a good picture as well; nor is that all, for in certain lights her father's country house is visible somewhere in the background as if painted in the varnish.

Philip Connard painted during the first half of this century and was the last of my great grandfather's protégés. A kindly gallery owner sent him to our home after he had gone the length of Bond Street with a cab full of his paintings, trying to interest gallery owners. He painted a very sympathetic portrait of my great grandfather showing him a portly, bespectacled and moustachioed man sitting on a small chair, looking up from a drawing he was examining, an open portfolio on another dining room chair in front of him, and behind him a diminishing enfilade of doors with regular splashes of sun on the floor by each unseen sash window: the room he sits in is rich red with the damask hangings favoured by Victorians. The picture is an exception to the ill usage meted out by portrait painters to portly Edwardian bankers. The usual portrait shows a mass of black broadcloth with highlights on the boots and tiepins. Sargent daringly carried the work into the realms of caricature as we see in his pictures of the Wertheimers and Pierrepont Morgan. My great grandfather's co-directors treated in this manner have all been since debooted and even debagged to allow more room for their successors in the boardrooms of the City.

We had at home a painting of the Brighton sea front by Eve Kirk, done with a palette knife and so good I have never wished to mar the pleasure it gives by seeing the original subject. I was able to buy two pictures by her, one of a harbour scene and the other of Fitzroy Square viewed from her studio, and this last picture includes a most unusual element rarely ever seen in serious painting; a motor car. I imagine the motor car is excluded because artists, by virtue of the difficulties of their profession, often own such loathsome vehicles that they lay by a stock of hate for the monster of our times and exclude it from their work. Eve Kirk seems to have painted very few pictures, usually with a palette knife, but she was never tempted into the realms of sculptural impasto which have been so successfully exploited by an artist called John (not, of course, Augustus) whose plastic contoured Portofinos are ubiquitous. The other John (Augustus, of course) praised Eve Kirk's work which is a considerable recommendation as he was not given to polite circumlocutions on such matters.

James McBey, the last of my four favourites, was best known as an etcher; if it is possible, he could be said to have started etching before he started drawing which may sound

ADDING TO THE HOARD

strange but the technical process is a fascinating world in itself. Recently he has been belatedly recognised as a consummate draughtsman and water colourist; pen and wash was his speciality. His mastery of line (I believe this to be the correct expression) is close to Rembrandt or Augustus John. I have always liked pen and wash because it combines strong indelible drawing that stands out across a room with the delightful colour effects of water colours neatly boxed up so they don't disappear into an evanescent haze at over two yards. This allows the pictures in this medium to be enjoyed across a room, whereas many water colours or drawings cannot stand so exposed and are best portfolioed. My mother was introduced to the artist by Martin Hardie and bought a pen and wash drawing that Hardie, himself no mean performer, had hoped to buy. It shows a North African fishing on the coast, an ordinary subject for an artist who lived at Tangier but it also shows the tug of the line in the fisherman's elbow; the rod and line he deemed superfluous and do not appear.

All this dawdling in the safe and certified pastures of connoisseurship does nothing for artists alive and painting now, and it is not the business of the collector to aggrandise the fortunes of picture dealers in Bond Street alone. He must go out into the byways and seek out the living artist. This is not always easy. Once, and only once, did everything go according to plan after I had seen a water colour I liked in an Academy exhibition. I wrote to the artist, was invited to tea (excellent), selected two water colours, was given two small trifles, paid my money, packed my pictures and left after a very pleasant afternoon. On two other occasions I have followed up pictures seen and enjoyed, tracked down the artists, bought pictures and gone home a happy man only to be let down by the painter, who has gone on to exploit the modestly successful vein they have opened up and degenerated into chocolate box lid manufacturers, ever weakening and watering down their talent. I do not like to deny an artist his livelihood, but I like to think of them striving and continuously developing their work; this is where portrait painting used to serve a useful purpose because this work supported the artist and gave him the time to do his own real work without damaging his reputation, because the portraits were hastily removed by their proud subjects to some distant and inert environment, never to endanger the artist's reputation again in his lifetime. Another sad case that illustrates this was the eminent water colourist Russell Flint, who discovered an insatiable demand for pictures of Spanish laundresses at work, déshabillé; only very rarely in his later years did he give evidence of his real brilliance: I remember a marvellous water colour of the Academy courtyard after a rainstorm, but ladies of Spain, I do not adore you.

Another danger is the man who only paints one good picture. I don't mind owning it, but the burden of upholding his reputation against all comers, single handed, is more than can be expected of the luckless owner. The 'Death of Chatterton' by Henry Wallis is a well-known example.

Then there is the artist who will not sell his pictures. I was much taken by a book of drawings for children done with adults in mind too; a good combination for a successful children's book because neither party are bored by reading it together. I found that the artist lived in easy bothering distance and telephoned. His wife was a most able defender of his peace and seclusion and tried first to put me off by refusing to believe I was anything other than a disguised collector of Value Added Tax. My alternately fruity and dulcet tones eventually settled this point, only

ADDING TO THE HOARD

to raise the spectre of the smart young gallery man on the make. This also I tried to refute and she eventually fell back, fighting a rearguard action, saying they were old and not well and so I capitulated. May he paint in peace!

I have made picture collecting sound very difficult, which it is: if there is a good rule to be followed it is to buy for pleasure and to buy on impulse. Good pictures are always snapped up quickly and if you delay the chance will not come again. Should the picture fail to please, you can always sell it.

You are not obliged to collect pictures; there are many other subjects. Furniture attracts many collectors and I have been tempted here too. There is a limit to the amount of furniture you can have in a house, and likewise a limit to its use: nothing is more horrible than a room packed with furniture for its own sake rather than use and comfort. In my own living room there is a circle of comfortable furniture round the fireplace: outside, round the walls of the room, stand the chaise longue, marble-topped consoles and walnut cabinets; fine looking but not so useful. Should this phalanx of pristine proportions invade the inner circle, comfort and ease have gone. This is why the furniture collector must be careful to think of utility when buying. A set of Chippendale ribbon-back dining room chairs in a large and busy family would require a resident cabinet maker; we forget that their original owners probably had one. On the other hand a glazed eighteenth century cabinet is quite man enough for its light duties to this day.

As I said, I have been tempted when the right and desired article has come along at a reasonable price. I long wanted a four poster bed but eventually found a half tester bed, property of a horsedealer, and this I secured for £11. It is an opulent Victorian piece in the pseudo-baroque taste of

THE DIVERSIONS

the 1850's and 60's, where every curve and line is a wilful distortion of the original style. It is imposing, magnificent, even comfortable, but coarse. It is as if the maker was saying 'I've as much mahogany as I want and a band saw. Look what I can do with it.' From another horsedealer I bought a set of eight Victorian gothic dining room chairs made of oak and not a single joint moving after 130 years of use. They too are covered with a lacework of amusingly ill-digested ornament but are so strong that the children play traffic and house games with them in rows on the polished oak floor of the dining room. They replaced a real collector's piece, a set of 6 French 'Restauration' (c.1820) chairs without a straight inch of wood or firm joint in them. From an antique dealer I bought a sofa, not for sitting on but for its quality; a boxy 2-seater, a late Victorian interpretation of one of Sheraton's patterns. No detail was left out; the cabinet maker repeated the design as crisply and clearly as the original engraving but in rosewood. I was lucky to buy it as it is the only piece of furniture of best quality I shall ever own. It would not be possible to have made it better and explodes the fallacy, once put about by a famous authority, that no good furniture was made in England after the death of George IV.

As a modest collector I had one coup on my own doorstep. An old man used to live in the village whose family had come down in the world, but they had kept their furniture. Of this the old man was justly proud and he showed me his things once. They had belonged to an early eighteenth century parson of the village and included a Cromwellian gate-leg table, a later mahogany flapped table, a fine long case clock with a brass and silvered dial and, best of all, a bureau in oak with four drawers under and a secret well, standing on six turned legs joined by

ADDING TO THE HOARD

a stretcher at the bottom. After his death I made enquiries. His heirs lived in Bournemouth and so did not want his things; a modest bid secured the entire contents of the house and his furniture has never left the village. I think he would have been pleased.

One of the failings of some collectors is that they stick to just one subject and will, for instance, contrive a very nice room of furniture which they mar with a tuppenny ha'penny clock and indifferent pictures. Presuming you have your furnishings and pictures, you will need the trimmings; those objets d'art scattered about the room and serving no obvious purpose other than to delight the eye. For my part I would settle for Chinese porcelain and renaissance bronzes, very lofty ambitions needing a lot of money and some specialist knowledge. Those of an economical turn of mind can buy Meissen shepherdesses and French ormulu. If I had my way, the time and the money, I would seek out Chinese vases of good form with lustrous crackled glazes running down the sides in irregular blobs and, since I am in the world of wishful thinking, I would like them ormulu mounted in the rococo taste but as you may well imagine, I will have to go without. As for my renaissance bronzes, I prefer these to doubtful great canvasses of the period. I would collect the portrait medallions so extensively produced at that period and which are an excellent way for the man in the street to come to grips with the great or nearly great artist. I looked into the subject; the books were few and not apparently concerned with the artistic quality of their subjects. This was my first disappointment. My second was the great dearth of the genuine article and so my ambitions have lapsed, which is a pity as a small cabinet of such things can store the quintessence of the renaissance; poisoners and Popes, scholars and scoundrels, all in one box, nearly indestructible and maintenance free; so much more handy than a marble hall filled with billowing and murky pictures.

Those who have never collected anything and are consequently indifferent to their surroundings must be much mystified by this subject; the gap between collectors and other people is very large. I shall not try to bridge it; I do not want to, because these others are a lost cause. May they revel in their lusty philistinism. On the other hand, to be carried too far, to become a curator and not a collector, is just as bad. As in most things, a middle course is best struck and maintained.

Eight
A Garden of Delight

'We must cultivate our garden' are the last words of one of the most influential books ever written. Philosophers rarely break down so far as to give practical advice, usually they are concerned with first causes and other tenuous abstractions: so we must snatch at Voltaire's advice and follow it as long as it is not too wet out of doors, for this advice banishes his three great evils – boredom, vice and poverty – in one sweep.

Once out of doors, Voltaire has little to offer the gardener by way of information and we must turn to more specific manuals. One of these was strangely influential in my own childhood. 'Three Little Gardeners' by L. Agnes Talbot, was published in the early years of the century, it had belonged to my mother and as she had three children, she decided to give us three gardens. The book shows pictures of the mob-capped, button-gaitered children of the period going about their work, month by month, and their relationship with the old family gardener. An identical worthy existed for us and treated us in the same kindly and condescending way. Our three little plots were side by side; mine grew at the expense of my neighbours, a reflection on my greed rather than my ability; my brother and sister were older and lost interest, as did I later, and they reverted to the care of the gardener. Years later I was furious to see my rockery removed although I had not looked at it for many seasons.

The garden we children grew up in had been laid out by my grandmother. Terraces of stonework and borders of herbaceous plants went down to a large lawn. Brick paths and yew hedges went from nowhere to nowhere and the whole overlooked a scrubby field. Furthermore, it was situated behind the house, which was too near the road and, all in all, was not the most successful of gardens. It was windy and devoid of any corner where one might be tempted to linger or sit out. The kitchen garden was more fun; little box hedges a foot high surrounded the vegetable beds, gnarled and botulous fruit trees grew here and there and a small, smelly stream ran at the bottom, passing through a nuttery.

Neither of my parents were very interested in the garden but they did like it kept tidy. This tidiness is easy to take for granted but it is the result of constant unobtrusive scraping and hoeing, which if neglected for a month is soon noticed. This uninspired pleasaunce was our playground and any real interest it may have had stemmed from the gardeners and they in turn were only interested in growing vegetables. For fifty years Arthur Lane reigned supreme. In appearance he resembled an Edwardian baronet; without hurry or fluster he got round the work, assisted by a homunculus called Ben Kelley, a wry taciturn man with a sharp sense of humour and mainly remarkable for wearing puttees into the 1970s. Was he the last World War I veteran to keep faithful to the uniform? In 1916 he had sustained some injury that had fixed him firmly in that period. He worked half the time in the woods as an unpaid, self-appointed keeper, although there was no shooting except on Boxing Day when the whole village went forth. In his woods he

A GARDEN OF DELIGHT

was king and happy; there he shot squirrels and magpies, hanging them up in a smelly keepers' rack and each night he returned home with a long crooked stick for his fire.

After Arthur Lane's retirement a new man came, in the prime of life and energetic – Ben Kelley retired to his woods. A weed's life was not worth a minute's purchase, bare earth girdles surrounded the trees and ate into the lawns. He certainly grew vegetables but eventually he abused the terms of his employment that allowed him to sell his surplus, by disposing of seed potatoes, so he went and was replaced by the present incumbent, a sturdy old countryman marvellously capable at playing off the disjointed members of our family against each other and so keeping us all on our toes. Old Ben Kelley emerged from his woods and joined up again. A third old countryman was also enrolled and they made a splendid team. The garden was no more interesting than before but the spectacle of three men bobbing about in a flower bed is more impressive than many floral displays. All the old men have retired or are dead; now a boy – we call him a boy but I believe he is over twenty-five – does the work and the old head-gardener potters about beside him.

So it was that I grew up without knowing how to dig. On moving to my present home I took on another of my grandmother's gardens. This one had been made in her retirement and was just grass and fruit trees. The lay-out was not well conceived, the wind whistles through it still; a wind-break should have been planted before the war but I am grateful for the fruit trees and am amazed at her consideration for future generations: who in their seventies plants a mulberry tree? She did and how good they are thirty years on.

We, that is my wife and I, have made it a rare stick

garden; she plans and I plant. Chalk is not the kindest soil to start rare shrubs and trees in; it has been done, as the readers of Sir F. Stern's book, 'A Chalk Garden', know. He was lucky enough to be sunk in an old chalk quarry while we are in an exposed and funnel-like valley. The idea is that the shrubs and trees will grow together to form well variegated masses of foliage. No longer will the mower have to thread its way through a maze of sticks as if it were in a bending race; the actual amount of lawn will be sensibly reduced as well. Our trees and shrubs have not been chosen for sudden and vulgar display but for consistent performance. They must have some flower, preferably not pink; an interesting shape, but not too lax and untidy; fruit if possible and autumnal colouring. The sort of tree held in poor esteem in our garden is the lilac; out of flower it is very dull, in flower the colours are questionable but fortunately short-lived. To list the names of all the rare sticks that do find favour would be tedious but I shall mention a few. 'The Sorbus' (White Beam) family do well on chalk and old Ben Kelley referred to the native downland type as a 'sort of a palm'. Maples likewise flourish although our 'Acer velutinum van volxemii' is too like a sycamore for comfort, but the name was a great temptation. 'Ptelea trifoliata aurea' is an obscure yellow American tree with wonderfully scented flowers and looks well against a deep green background. 'Cornus controversa variegata', the prize of any tree and shrub garden, grows slowly on in a special place. 'Hoheria glabrata', an evergreen tree from New Zealand with delicate white flowers, grew with such abandon that it even surprised the nursery man who supplied it. We have a 'Malus tschonoskii', the crab apple with everything, including red buds in winter, and 'Clerodendro bungei', a foul-smelling wall shrub with flat, plum-coloured flower heads in August and September when little else flowers amongst the shrubs. These are the sort of rare sticks we grow and one day it is hoped that they will grow together and snake round about the garden forming trouble-free shrubberies, with nooks and crannies behind them and paths going nowhere in particular like all the best paths.

Because of the peculiarities of the site and the lie of the land, I am not able to make a garden to suit my own tastes and ideas. These are not very original as many gardens exist that would suit me. To one side of the Petit Trianon at Versailles is an excellent example: a rectangular lawn enclosed by hedges and lightly-trimmed limes, not limes with the leprous digits so favoured by the over-enthusiastic pruner, but the red barked sort allowed to show colour in winter from the young twigs. At one end I would have a colonnade with a little room behind and at the other end would be a view, not a vast three counties and ten steeples affair, but a more intimate view – a field or two, cattle, trees and maybe a bit of a distant hill. A vast and extensive vista is a mistake, as it invites all the winds that blow to come and do so.

Enough of these dreams; I have my business and calling in the vegetable garden and here I am in charge. I have several vegetable gardens. The first is a little square behind the stable for salads, courgettes and herbs. The stable wall has five apples and four pears trained on it. A fan-trained Comice is the centre-piece and fruits well. I bought an apple called a Pitmaston Pineapple, purely because of the name; the fruit was an unexpected bonus. Tomatoes and gooseberries grow in the blank spaces under the windows. My second plot lies a little further off and is given over to roots, peas, artichokes, sorrel, broccoli and other vegetables of the sort that cooks like to rush out and pick in a moment of inspiration. Two standard pears and a quince lend a bit of shade to an otherwise flat and dull bit of ground. The pears are Jargonelle, a summer ripening fruit, and a Black Worcester, a large, keeping cooker; again bought because the name was amusing. The quince has been slow to come to fruition and could have well been planted as an ornamental shrub elsewhere; along with the mulberry and medlar it is part of the neglected orchard triumvirate. All three trees should be planted more often, if only for looks, but they enable the cook to embellish and vary the winter diet of cooking apples. I also grow flowers for cutting in this plot of ground. The reader will have noticed the absence of flower beds; we have one of spring bulbs, paeonies and what plantsmen call sub shrubs and that is all – as well as enough. The colours required for floral decoration inside a house are so different from what I want to see out of doors in the garden where I am not keen on raucous blossom, as you may have gathered! These more flamboyant hues are confined to the vegetable garden in rows, like cabbages.

My main crops are grown in a field, through the kindness of a nearby farmer, and I would recommend anybody with a farm or good neighbour to do likewise as it takes all the back-breaking toil out of the business of providing enough food for the year, or keeping a gardener. The system is this: the farmer has a field left fallow in summer to clean it, and this field doubtless has a corner or two of no great merit or importance. Here I spread my horse manure (q.v. my notes on 'The Chase'); the tractors plough and cultivate it to a good tilth and I come along with half a hundredweight of seed potatoes and five hundred onion sets, dib them in and go away for a month. I then return and hoe the young weeds out, earth up the potatoes, plant the french beans, cabbages, peas etc., and then go away for another month. After a little more weeding it is all picking, and at the end of the year the plough eradicates the mess I have made. I have neighbours too, as the farmer allows other people patches beside me. It is not unlike allotments and I imagine we share some of the long summer evening camaraderie that I hope exists in such places. The farmer has a share too, and so everybody benefits. It enables me to grow the bulk of my vegetable needs and as I grow more than I require, I can feed the numerous pests much written about by gardening correspondents in newspapers; this seems simpler than fiddling about with all those awful poisons. Such are the benefits of living in a balanced and friendly community.

The purist will criticize this scheme as not real gardening, but a keen gardener usually has limited space and lots of time and enthusiasm. I have unlimited space and a great many other things to do, so I take as many short-cuts as possible. I am in gardening for food, not for the love of tilling the soil. As to our ornamental garden, here too the work is kept to a minimum, just mowing and one flower bed; to do more would defeat the object of the garden and exhaust its custodian. It is hard to enjoy a really neat garden because some little imperfection is always aggravating the owner, nor can you enjoy it exhausted and sweaty from the work of keeping it tidy. So it is we have plenty of weeds, plenty of food and plenty of time – not to mention some very rare sticks.

Nine
'Of Books there is no End'

We are assured, by those who collect statistics on such matters, that illiteracy is a beaten bogey; the written word is everywhere triumphant. This may be the happy state at which we have arrived, but all is not well elsewhere; there seems to be a marked reluctance of the many, so well equipped, to exercise their skills in this direction. In short, the decline in reading has become as general as the skill that makes it possible; a very sad state of affairs. The blame can be put on the great cost of better books and the influence of television. I do not want to be nasty about the latter, but the tastes and interests that go towards making a person 'well read' are too varied to be successfully covered by this form of communication: it may not be pitched at the lowest denominator but it certainly has to consider the commonest. An instance of this is the performing arts, which are ideally suited to television, people's interests change to what is laid before them. The other arts, decorative, applied or just pure art, are in decline as people opt for what they can see at home. The phrase 'well read' has an old fashioned sound about it; it is rarely used and people so described are becoming rarer too.

In the world of books and reading there are infinitely numerous combinations; never have there been more titles on offer to fewer purchasers: the words of the preacher 'Of making many books there is no end' is very true today and I am doing nothing to improve the situation by writing this, nor am I put off by the next line 'And much study is a weariness of the flesh'. The reader of today does not seem to champ through enough books, and I am sure one of the reasons for this is that he does not have all his books by him for reference and occasional dipping. To become well read through a public library is difficult, as the hours of reading and library opening are not compatible except to the student or pensioner. He does not have his own books by him because he is always moving house; this twentieth century vice is very hard on books, it is always the books that are left behind or disposed of elsewhere.

Reading habits are a strangely neglected subject. The great din and prattle about education rarely pauses for any consideration of the matter, yet the acquisition of regular reading habits is surely half the battle won. There is a laudable desire on the part of the educators that their pupils should acquire the skill, but little is done to further the habit thereafter. An educated person with an enquiring mind will spend more time reading than any other occupation with the exception of sleeping. Let us imagine a civil servant and his daily routine: he peruses his paper during breakfast if it is allowed and delivered, he continues to read it in the train to work; at his office, much of his time is spent reading documents and memoranda; on the way home he looks over some papers and later that night he might read a book for an hour or two. By the time he goes to bed he will have spent six hours reading, some of it admittedly in the course of duty, but all in all a very substantial part of the day is spent in front of the printed word. How is he to survive such a heavy bombardment? He must develop a critical faculty and this is achieved by reading a great deal indiscriminately at some time in his life. Anybody who has

THE DIVERSIONS

done this will find that most of what he reads is absolute rubbish, a little is just rubbish, and a tiny proportion is well worth reading. His critical faculty should enable him to forget the dross and remember those things worth keeping, but he must have a good memory, this being an essential part of a well educated person; without it he cannot hope to aspire to that title. He can be a useful member of society, a prop and stay of his community, but never an educated man. I am afraid I must dismiss the mass of mankind for having little or no memory at all, nor can I hold out any hopes of their cultivating any. You are born with a good memory and have probably inherited it. Suggesting this is a heresy of considerable dimensions to some people. All too often you hear somebody describe something they have read in a newspaper; they go off at a fine canter, remembering not what they have read but that they have read something, and soon they stumble into silence having forgotten all the details, closing their remarks with the words 'You know what I mean, don't you?' which being probably the case, it would have been better if they had spared you their impressions of the matter.

I can see no remedy for this sad state of affairs except that we go into the library and close the door firmly behind us. I use the word library to describe the books I have read rather than those I own. I always try to own books I have enjoyed and a little hunting around in second-hand bookshops usually provides the sought-after book. Some people seem strangely satisfied to read a book and then return it to the lending library without a qualm. They do not consider the possibility of having a copy by, for rereading or reference at a later date.

I learnt to read at an ordinary age and made no great use of this skill until I was eight years old when I read a short

'OF BOOKS THERE IS NO END'

story set in Mayan Central America of all unlikely places, and from that moment onwards I was devoured by an insatiable curiosity to know more; it was as if I was an electrical device and had been switched on. These moments of burgeoning intellectual awareness are very vital moments in a person's life and I can recall this one quite clearly. The boy expert on the other hand is a well known and trying phenomenon. I was spared the usual odium heaped on such people because my subject was too remote to attract attention. I was liberally supplied with books by a father indulgent in this respect alone and did accumulate a great mass of information on pre-Colombian American history. Had my energies been directed towards my school work, I might have made some mark as a scholar, but I didn't. My mind was far too busy unveiling overgrown temples in the tangled jungles of the Yucatan and no doubt I infuriated my teachers, as any supposedly intelligent child does who is immune to their influence. I was ten years growing out of this stuff but I did not regret it as I was able to survey a subject, albeit small and distant, very deeply from top to bottom and side to side and can now, when approaching a new interest, apply the subject handling skills I learnt in that remote and solitary study. In short I developed a critical faculty which, as I never went to a university where they teach out of the way subjects for this reason, has stood me in good stead. The other books I read at preparatory school were novels by Conan Doyle, Rider Haggard, John Buchan and suchlikes. The library was unkempt and unloved; there seemed to be no policy for filling the shelves with books or inducing the boys to read them. There was, of course, the usual complicated system of entering books as they were taken out to be read, completely unnecessary in the closed community of a school: a school, I may say, that had a high opinion of itself, substantial fees and twice the responsibility of royalty (foreign, of course). These impoverished facilities always surprised me until I moved to an even more expensive school where they were infinitely worse. The so-called library was in a senior common room, in itself a considerable deterrent for a bookish little boy. But worse, these treasures were kept under lock and key, the heavy grilles prevented me from seeing even the titles of the books. I was told that they had been left behind by the last private owner of the house, he having no use for them. Elsewhere in this most expensive of schools (always to the front in this respect) was a collection of war escape stories given by a retired member of the kitchen staff and a copy of Winston Churchill's book on the Duke of Marlborough, which I can only imagine had been won in a raffle. Such was the library and I nearly gave up reading altogether.

Once released from school my natural curiosity reasserted itself and I came to patronise a very particular sort of library, now becoming rarer, the second hand book shop with a literate proprietor. These unsung tutors of the footloose reader deserve more praise than is usually given them. I would exalt them well above the municipal librarian who is overconcerned with what he has in his shelves, and where it is; something that never seems to worry the second hand dealer in books. They helped guide my reading at a time when it had no directing influence. I had by this time cast off the rigid shackles of my pre-Colombian studies and broadened my interests to include history, art, travel, biography and the ludicrously named 'belles lettres'.

To list the titles of all the books I have read and enjoyed would be an unpardonable rudeness although proving me a well read pedant at the same time, but as we are in the

'OF BOOKS THERE IS NO END'

library and needs must notice our favourite books, no one would quibble if I said that a favourite book is one you turn to again and again without disappointment. The very notion will strike terror into the hearts of the book shy but cause no comment in the present company.

I think of books in batches or cliques of like-minded volumes and shall offer only a few parcels for your consideration. The first bundle includes Montaigne, Gibbon's autobiography, Osbert Sitwell's memoirs and a group of early Russian books. Montaigne came to me through Virginia Woolf's essay in the Common Reader, that consummate introduction to many good friends. I still do not know if it is the rosy impression her essay created, or the actual Montaigne that I like, but I keep pushing on, dodging the thickets of obscure classical quotation, determined to enjoy it and often rewarded. It requires perseverance as a bad portion would put off a weak reader for life and there are bad bits and plain dull bits, rescued from oblivion by flashes of fire and enlightenment. The author steps forward so modern in his manner that meeting him on a bus would cause no surprise.

Sir Osbert Sitwell's memoirs are a luxurious pilgrimage through the recent past viewed from the Gothick battlements of an intelligent baronetcy; our age of the commonplace is thrust away from the reader, this is no book for the egalitarian. One of these, recently reviewing the book, tore it to pieces because the writer and his father employed servants, a most peculiar criterion for judging literature. The more balanced reader will find the finest description extant of life before the collapse of civilization in 1914, this date always being given for that event by the ever dwindling survivors of that period. The book is a successful argument for civilization; not the politician's civilization, nor that of the industrialist, but pure civilization, a fragile and rather effete flowering so easily trampled underfoot by forces much in evidence today. Were I to lay money on literary fortunes, this is a book I would back as the best work of that most fecund of literary families. As for the author, we know what he did, the how and why, but we can gather very little about himself; he is far less explicit than Montaigne in this respect, although the latter was writing about things other than himself.

Gibbon's great and meaty history overshadows his autobiography, a neat little book with which the writer took great pains. It describes an uneventful life so necessary for the completion of his huge work of scholarship; the quiet and steady progress of his work looms through the book and provides the interest and theme which it otherwise lacks. It is also a charming description of eighteenth century life and a prelude to the works of Jane Austen; the atmosphere of the book is similar to those novels.

My Russians include Gogol's 'Dead Souls', a leisurely journey among the landowners of Russia. His Russia has changed and gone, but my neighbours are all there and I can recognise them one by one as I read the book. Aksakov's 'A Family History' is a less well known book; the thousand pages would deter many publishers and translators, but the work has been done and done well. It describes life in Russia on a remote estate, the interest and charm (I speak as an out of doors man) overlaid with a veneer of civilization usually lacking in such situations. Strange to relate, the effect made by the book is not too distant from the picture of Irish country life given us by Somerville and Ross in the 'Memoirs of an Irish R.M.'. Turgenev's 'Sportsman's Notes' is a book that describes a similar scene; the author's sporting experiences in a land blessedly free from the British game laws and that unpleasant preoccupation with enormous bags of game. His philosophical vein is muted in this book which is not a bad thing, as some of his books share the faults of Aldous Huxley's novels where the characters preach overmuch and eventually forget to play their parts in the story. How Turgenev must have yearned to relive these experiences in later life when he lived in Paris in that very indoor society that one associates with writers.

With the exception of Gibbon and Turgenev these are big books, and a good big book is vastly superior to a small one; it is like having good friends to stay rather than just for supper, you are able to live for weeks on terms of easy familiarity with the families and people described. It is difficult to write exactly about these books and the pleasure they give. They are books of atmosphere, not action, and unless constantly re-read it is easy to forget the exact and often modest contents; the reader is left with a rosy impression and little else. I will admit to being very partial to these re-creations of squirearchial life. The authors in this selection were all landowners, with the possible exception of Gibbon who made the whole Roman Empire his own; they demonstrate the correct and balanced life that can be lived by an intelligent person in decent and healthy surroundings. It is very self indulgent but pleasant to read improved editions of one's own life freed from the many small daily vexations, the leaking roofs and rising damp. I can escape into their well run rural paradises, forget the mud outside and enjoy their conversation.

Reading is not all pure escapism; pleasure and profit can be combined if you tackle something more meaty. You might think that Gibbon's great history rather than his autobiography is an answer but it is too specialized. I suspect that most are unaware that the book is about Constantinople; its title is a deceit, as who gives a brass farthing for the thousand years of dwindling power and internecine strife that occurred well outside our world, especially when there is so much history that has greater bearing on us today. By all means read the first volume but stop after that. Where our forefathers once resorted to Gibbon, we can take refuge in the even more extensive work of one of his admirers, A. J. Toynbee. You have to be a bold man to embark on this, for not only is the book enormous but it is generally discredited in academic circles; but do not be dismayed. It is written in English. Treat it as a world history. I have not the erudition to criticise his theories and am prepared to pass them by. There are many other things in the book, including philosophy and literature. I have reached Volume 5. Is this a record for a Common Reader? Death has now stopped the author's pen; formerly it raced ever onwards with reconsiderations and additions, faster than I progressed with the reading, but now I can catch up with some hope of winning. Some of the academic disapproval comes from his trespassing in a grand manner on small corners of history that some prickly specialist has made his own. This they do not relish, especially if their little world is exposed to the gaze of the vulgar. It is very necessary that writers like A. J. Toynbee should compound and distil such a vast amount of learning from erudite papers, rare books and odd sources, for how else are we, Virginia Woolf's Common Readers, to come at such a mass of interesting information so well set out? People who despise the 'vulgarisateur' forget the enormous intellectual abilities that men like Toynbee and Macaulay bring to history. There is as much distance between Toynbee and an ordinary historian, fussing about his little period, as

'OF BOOKS THERE IS NO END'

there is between that specialist and the man in the street. In power of memory alone the Toynbees and Macaulays are infinitely better able to sift, dismiss or include information as they encounter it and I for one am happier to have it as a good clear story, even if errors do exist in the details.

Having dealt with escapist reading and good heavy reading, I come to the most pernicious sort of reading; that which just fills in time. Various grades of this exist. At one end are the light and identical novels set in Cornish manor houses; they amuse that portion of the reading public that have not yet successfully thrown off the habit of reading through the influences of television and radio. My own taste in wasting time with a book is reading biographies and diaries. Diaries are particularly good for this purpose, as they are often extensive and can be picked up and put down with no danger that the story will get muddled because there is no story, as in Parson Woodforde's diary. Little or nothing ever happened to that worthy incumbent; his even, quiet and well fed life stretched over many decades; once you are well settled in the rectory (available in five volumes) you sink into his quiet life and long for the small excitements, excitements which in our own lives would cause no comment. I look forward to the recurring favourites of his table, for instance 'rabbits smothered in onions' (a culinary preparation rather than the mode of despatch!). All in all it is an excellent lavatory book. Kilvert, that other diary bound parson, I cannot abide and I returned my copy to the bookseller as soon as I could; it was all primroses and little girls. I believe there is even a society for his propagation, may they forgive me but I still think him a wet. The diaries of people who have actually done something are not necessarily more interesting than those of regular scribbling parsons, but are best considered as autobiographies or memoirs. Historical details can be picked up and the keen reader of this sort of book is always building up a picture of the period he is reading about. Old friends from other books pop in for a page or two and are gone again and there comes a time when the reader feels he has lived in good literary, commercial or political society, as the case may be, all his life. A complete picture of a period is stored away in his memory, but to what purpose?

For pleasure I will allow you to resort to novels but not thrillers. These are always disconcerting (for such is their purpose) but it is a poor thing if a story has to rely on eventfulness and suspense to provide pleasure. I doubt if they even aim to provide that; titillation is their object and I do not enjoy being gripped with suspense or taken by surprise. My life is not so dull as to need these stimulants, so it is that I am happy to read a novel where the spirit dominates over the body and its various functions! The novel by which I compare others is Evelyn Waugh's trilogy, 'Officers and Gentlemen'; his lighter novels are amusing and one can only regret that their success and resulting prosperity curtailed the writing of more serious novels. I grudge no writer his living but the affluent, check-tweeded and clarety decline of this author is a sad thing to read about in the various memoirs that have appeared since his death and it is a horrible antithesis to the dignified decline of Guy Crouchback's father, creeping genteely from his feudal splendours down to a seaside lodging house and part time teaching.

Another type of novel I enjoy is those I am tempted to call 'the bore you stiff school'. I feel I am being bored but obviously am not, for books can be easily put down. I am kept at them by the very suspense I have maligned in thrillers; but it is not the suspense of waiting for something ghastly to happen, it is waiting for anything to happen, and when it does, it is mentioned in such a low key that I can read a page or two and not notice. Ford Madox Ford's 'Good Soldier' is an example of this school, likewise Elizabeth Bowen's books and Antony Powell's huge duodecology: his characters philosophise more modestly than Aldous Huxley's, the raconteur's self effacement is marvellous and I suspect very necessary. A huge cast shuffle on and off with even less purpose than the extras in Dickens and I can only imagine that the author's object is to show how, like in our own lives, numerous people come and go leaving little trace behind. Like most other readers I was sustained by the prospect of Widmerpool's comeuppance.

I do not read many novels and perhaps unadventurously like to have them set in that portion of society to which I imagine I belong. This sounds a most reprehensible vice but social realism doesn't give you that self satisfying titillation if you live in a working class community. There is no thrill in peeping through the hole in the fence at other people's lives; the 'simple annals of the poor' are abundant and fresh if you live in an agricultural community. Most novels are set in those portions of society midway between the poor and the rich, and these hold no charm for me as they are usually set in towns and suburbs. There used to be a class of novels describing the vapid activities of titled people, but this school of writing was killed dead by P. G. Wodehouse's novels; now you can have your earls and laugh at them if you so desire. However I am now without a favourite living author; Evelyn Waugh is dead, Antony Powell has called a more than temporary halt; a runner-up, Simon Raven, mars his novels with overdrawn sexual fantasies aimed at increasing his sales.

Authors, please take note of this untapped market and write accordingly!

The bookish battlefield from which I fled a beaten man is that of the classics – Shakespeare, Dickens and other great names. I am always amazed that some people seem entirely satisfied with them and never stray into the byeways and I envy them in their luck of having so much, so well written to enjoy. As far as I am concerned, the faults of the classics lie with the reader and that of course is myself. I will not join Tolstoy in that unseemly battle of the giants and denigrate Shakespeare; I am sure the fault is mine. The modest performances I have seen are too full of ranted lines and purple hose; furthermore, by some ill luck, it is always the same two or three plays that come my way. In Dickens I am disconcerted by the huge and ever-expanding cast; halfway through the book still more troop in to initiate their little stories, only to be cast off in a chapter or two, leaving the reader wondering what to do with them. I am told that they are likely to all rush on stage in the last act and confuse me further. On the other hand I lately had some success with Jane Austen and found myself telling somebody, in tones of honeyed patronage, that she was a surprisingly good writer. I was reading 'Emma'; it is an extraordinary performance, to inflate the domestic trivia of a quiet provincial town into a great novel. Here I ran into an unexpected difficulty with that dyspeptic valeditudinarian, Mr Woodhouse, who shared the name of a slight acquaintance. My Mr Woodhouse was a substantial person, a desperate man across country on a horse. I should imagine he eats well and, if he will forgive me saying so, is noisy. I could not reconcile the two Woodhouses and it jarred every time the name was mentioned. I imagine authors have great difficulty in choosing the names of their principal characters;

they must be neither common, and so muddling us with Smiths and Browns we already know, nor too rare as in a novel of Ford Madox Ford's, where even the pronunciation is obscure. Jane Austen was just unlucky with her Woodhouse for me. It would seem that to be a successful writer you have to appeal to two different types of reader. The first and more numerous is perhaps not a very critical sort of reader but one able to know a good tale when met. This sort of reader boosts the sales and brings a smile to the publisher's face: the second sort is the literary nit picker; if your books pass their scrutiny and they are unable to fault you on any account, then you have a chance because they, too, enjoy a good read when they have put away their criticisms. The last important factor is scale: you must write plenty so you can become a regular habit with your readers.

I am very fond of travel books and have some qualification to speak of this sort of writing; the reader has encountered my idiosyncratic taste in literature, borne with my select and lofty sentiments on the novel and listened, I hope sympathetically, to my failure with the classics. I once conscientiously read through every travel book available in English on that part of South America which I will loosely call the Guianas, in the north east corner of the continent. I started with Sir Walter Raleigh's magnificent 'Discoverie of Guiana' and ended in a plethora of adventurous nonsense books. The result was that I found the good travel book a rare thing; about five in every hundred are good. Also, I discovered that the more remote and empty the traveller's terrain, the greater his skill will have to be to make it interesting. People are often tempted to travel to remote and uncharted places; this misguided curiosity is stimulated by the hope of finding something exceptional:

however, blank spaces on the map are usually blank because there is nothing there. This rule does not apply to scientific travellers who have good cause to go to such places; their difficulty is how not to overweight the book with specialised information best kept to a learned journal. A clever writer can unload quite a lot of this material but has to be very subtle in so doing. Some writers cast away in barren tracts have had to resort to the most desperate expedients. Peter Fleming in his 'Brazilian Adventure' turned on his fellow travellers and wrought a fine farce for us. Lesser writers in their books rely on descriptions of natural and physical horrors; the carnivorous piranha fish are rarely left out of any book on the Amazon basin: so consistently are their dangers enlarged on that I am tempted to write a travel book just to ignore them, although I was not unmindful of my toes when in those waters. That publishers should continue to print these collections of travellers' tales is a great mystery. I recollect one book by an arrant piffler who referred sententiously to his account as his 'literary labours', and still the publisher printed it. The most annoying thing about this type of author is that just sometimes they say something interesting and you have to read the book in case this happens.

The moment the traveller reaches more civilised lands things look up. The presence of vanished empires immeasurably enhances a book and we in England can now enjoy the double satisfaction of reading a book on the Middle East or India, written at the beginning of the century, where our own now vanished empire is shown imposed on somebody else's. The nostalgia is as a consequence very considerable and even mere travel books have charm as a period piece. We follow, for instance, the activities of a sportsman in the Himalayas, wrestling good humouredly

'OF BOOKS THERE IS NO END'

with his difficulties, refreshed by hampers of champagne borne uncomplainingly by porters to some ridiculous pole of inaccessibility. One such was Henry Savage Landor, grandson of the poet, an insufferable little cock sparrow of a man dancing about above the 23,000 ft. contour line in a straw boater and Norfolk jacket. He nearly came to grief because he would attack the whole Tibetan army, single handed but for two servants and one of those a leper. Such books are the background for the novels of John Buchan and Rider Haggard.

Travel books are still a neglected branch of literature; many great writers wrote them as well as lesser people who at some later date thought their experiences worth preserving. The act of travelling has prompted people to write books who otherwise would not have dreamt of putting pen to paper: these 'one off' writers have sometimes written unexpectedly good books; it is easy to imagine a retired district commissioner, bored by the quiet world of his retirement, reliving the excitements of his foreign service. Good writers seem loath to travel these days but before the war no faraway place was safe from observant and amusing writers.

Some readers may find my selections peculiar. The classics I have dismissed in a few words. Poetry and very modern writing are unmentioned; I do not ignore them but have not read enough to offer even the most rudimentary opinions. The mass of books available is so large that no one reader can hope to cover it all, even in the most superficial manner. Perhaps the 'well read' person is extinct because of this; his latter day successor can only show a patchy knowledge of what has been written, interspersed with huge gaps. Pleasure and information are what the reader should seek to accumulate. Slowly he builds up a vast mass of irrelevant information. The years go by, connecting links are made between subjects, people or things. Groping in the gloom he sees a picture forming of the world he lives in; it will never be complete. To this he is resigned but it is an image all the same, if only an outline. Should this outline be formed before senility or forgetfulness intervene, then you have an educated man, the finest product of our civilization; a man who has a balanced view of things, not given to violent enthusiasms, probably touched with more than a little cynicism, but balanced withal, and that in itself is no mean achievement.

Ten
The Chase

It is right and proper that an able bodied man should follow some outdoor sport that tests to the limits his courage, endurance and dexterity. Few would argue with this statement as it is very obvious, but I think it worth while to look a little further and not just dismiss it on the grounds that fitness alone calls for all this exercise. In man's primaeval condition any falling off of fitness resulted in hunger which, unless made good, caused a further deterioration and eventual death. In primitive societies the blind and chronically handicapped are condemned to the professions; poet and witchdoctor are their equivalents to our entertainers and doctors. Everybody else had to wrestle, fight and play. When we compare the interminable aeons of man's existence in this hearty primitive condition with our last few thousand years of relative sophistication, it would not be wrong to imagine that there is an inherited aggressiveness, a suppressed savagery in most of us and it needs must be let out for the good of our constitution. This is what sport is about, and so it is that regular attendance upon our chosen activity draws off all these nasty or uncouth primaeval instincts that would be unwelcome in our refined and delicate society today. It is no surprise then to realise that in those superbly evoked reconstructions of primitive society, the English boarding schools, sport is a paramount activity. The need remains even after our school days and happy is the man who has found his particular sport and the means whereby to indulge in it. When I say sport I mean something more active than the sedentary executive's Saturday afternoon of golf; I mean something much more exhausting and perhaps dangerous, something that tires, stretches to breaking point and often frightens the participant.

Looking back it seems that, for my part, a series of chance circumstances alone prompted me towards the Chase rather than ice hockey or hang gliding. On leaving agricultural college I was in the right condition to take up riding as I had never been soured by early experiences, nor did I have a daunting cavalry colonel for a father; I did have the time and the fields to keep the horse, but not the slightest inkling of an inclination in that direction. How then was the vital spark struck? A person's interests and hobbies are usually started by some unexpected and very spark-like flash of enlightenment or enthusiasm. In my case it was seeing a film called the 'List of Adrian Massinger'. I forget now who he was or why he had a list or what he even did with it, but I have not forgotten the long fox hunting sequence in which the bad man eventually came to grief jumping a stone wall and landing on a hay tedder. Apart from this last scene it looked good fun. The seed was sown and a year or two later it germinated when I happened to be in the public house at home where I said that I would like a horse 'to ride around the place on'. Fortunately there was at the bar an honest horse dealer and he volunteered to provide a suitable horse should he encounter one. We went our various ways and after a respectable pause he telephoned to say he had just such a horse. I suspect he had a stable of them all along but observed a decorous pause for effect; so, in due course, I was provided with an elderly, wall-eyed, grey gelding for £95, saddle and bridle included.

THE CHASE

At first I did not aspire to go hunting; to remain mounted was my main hope and I crept cautiously round lanes and fields, occasionally surveyed by an old retired groom who cast a kindly eye on my circlings and seat. Later lessons gave me the confidence to enjoy myself.

Then and only then did it seem possible to go hunting. We lived on the edge of a hunting country and were quite out of touch with such matters but had known somebody whose husband had been the Master of the local pack; enquiries revealed that the sport not only survived but that I would be most welcome. Thereafter I was initiated into the Chase; my experiences and fears were identical to Siegfried Sassoon's as described in his memoirs and so I shall not try to rival his excellent descriptions except to say that my first meet was cancelled on account of fog and that my Lord Dumborough was a much kinder man who impressed me greatly by taking off his glove to shake hands, a refinement of good manners that had not occurred to me before.

If you have not followed hounds you will not know what I am writing about, so I shall describe the sport. The huntsman takes the hounds to a wood or overgrown place where he thinks a fox may be lying up for the day as is their wont. The field or mounted followers are put safely on one side as they are of little real use and only out for pleasure. They are placed so as not to interfere with the line the fox may take, bearing in mind the direction of the wind and the way it is hoped the fox will go, for preference across a good bit of riding country free from railways, roads and barbed wire fences. The hounds stir the fox from his lair, he leaves and the hounds are then encouraged to pursue him across country. The field, possibly led by a small girl out of control, or, failing that, the masters, set off in pursuit of the hounds; never, I must add, the fox. The fox is surprisingly fast and knows where he is going. If the scent is good the hounds follow him unerringly up hill and down dale and the riders endeavour to do likewise. Depending on the type of country and length of the run, the field dwindles. Some fall off and have to catch their horses, others find the work too much for their horses, yet others are unable to clear the obstacles encountered. Sometimes there is a check when hounds miss or over-run the scent and those left behind can catch up. The huntsman does his best to lay the hounds on the scent again and the chase is renewed. Maybe by now only the most determined riders are left, an esprit de corps suddenly develops, risks are taken, gates flown and broken, hedges jumped with no knowledge of what is on the other side. Horses and humans alike are strained to their utmost and eventually one of three things can happen; the fox is caught in the open and is eaten, or he goes into a hole where he is left as inaccessible, or coaxed out by the terriers, shot and given to the hounds. Sometimes the scent just peters out, cannot be found again and so is given up.

The skills and pleasure are these; riding as fast and skilfully as possible, at the same time watching the hounds and, if very lucky, the fox as well, comparing the two courses they take, or admiring hounds if there is only one: you are probably reckoning where the fox has gone, if he is out of sight and taking short cuts, but you must never get mixed up with hounds. Your ambition is to arrive at the end of the hunt (in as small and select company as possible) in one piece on your own horse. You jump off, loosen the girths to ease your perspiring steed and discuss your adventures in a modest manner with only a few guarded exaggerations.

So it is that I am a fox hunter, a much maligned but sturdy minority. Now for the reasons why I and many

THE CHASE

others persist in our folly. It can be said with assurance that the sport offers more than most others. I do not wish to appear competitive in this respect, and denigrate simpler pastimes, but I find that the more work you put into your sport the more you will get out of it. Even to arrive at a meet requires a great deal of work and many ancillary skills, as varied as knowing how to drive a lorry, maintain a large and delicate animal in good condition, clean innumerable appurtenances and recognise left from right handed spurs; let alone knowing how to ride. Sound wind and a pair of gymshoes is not enough for this sport. It panders to so many different sides of human nature: the thrill of the chase, a taste for company, exercise, seeing the countryside, even sartorial pride, all these interests can be indulged in to perfection.

The 'thrill of the chase' is the principal attraction of the sport and it would seem that this means being well and truly frightened. I will not indulge in tuppenny psychology, but it is plain that people like to take risks, preferably small and numerous rather than large and occasional and derive therefrom some pleasure; at least the fox hunters endanger no innocent bystander. It was not for nothing that Surtees through his Mr Jorrocks likens the sport to war, with but a small portion of its dangers. For the fox hunter can share the exultation of a cavalry charge or the restlessness of the Mongol hordes all in his own home county. As to being frightened, all of us except the wholly unimaginative share this to a greater or lesser extent; one person is terrified of jumping hedges, another stout rails and most of jumping spreads of water where, strange to say, the risk is least. My own particular dislike is a small crowded rail surrounded by impatient horses. There are people who seem frightened of everything and they would do well to go home, if only for the sake of their horse's nerves; for the horse, while not the most intelligent of domestic animals, is very perceptive and smells fright even before his rider has gathered his funk up together. The bond between rider and mount can be very close and satisfying for both parties and great things can be achieved in this condition of togetherness. Many riders never seem to come to this degree of trust, a trust that clears cattlegrids at a canter and other dangerous exploits. It is a question of sympathy rather than sophistication in the saddle.

As for the taste for company, we are assured that man is a gregarious creature and a famous wit had very hard things to say about the company in question and I will admit to encountering people out hunting with whom even the most superficial banalities are an effort. There are also those who extend their talks to include the HORSE, a noble animal indeed, but not a staple of decent conversation. There are, however, many interesting people outside the scope of Wilde's encomiums. I recollect enjoying the conversation of a footwear manufacturer to such an extent that I ignored the departure of the fox on his travels. I was much taken by surprise at another aspect of our gregarious nature that I first met on the hunting field, namely team spirit. A lot is said about it at schools and by those who play games; not being an enthusiast for games, I had missed out on it but it proved a congenial emotion and the loss had been mine. In the foxhunting field it is a looser tie than in a rugger team, but it exists all the same and is best seen when the riding is hard and the numbers few, select and choice occasions! I cannot believe my school teachers were such subtle psychologists as to provide this receptacle for youthful emotions and rumbustious spirits on purpose. No, it would seem that we need some group to which we can pledge our fealty outside our family circle; sometimes it is a club, or a regiment or even a pub. Whatever the group is, it is the object of certain imperfect emotions that find no place in the family circle. Do not imagine that I propose that all who support such institutions are emotionally deprived; their families are lucky that certain manifestations of their character, especially the aggressive sort, are dissipated elsewhere and the amateur anthropologist in me puts all this down to the vestiges of tribal sentiment.

Doubtless you have seen in newspapers the advertisements for a loathsome contraption, the picture showing a lissom and seductive woman leaning back from a stanchion supported by a large elastic band, the idea being that it vibrates her yet thinner. Likewise bicycles can be obtained that go nowhere with great effort and these achieve the same effect. The horse is an excellent substitute for these gadgets and can be used out of doors without attracting the ridicule that would surely come your way otherwise. There are numerous sayings that bear this out, indicating that the outside of the horse is good for the inside of man and that days spent hunting are not counted by Allah. All these indicate the obvious excellence of the horse as a means of exercise. Need I say more except to add that a day's hunting denies you a superfluous midday meal as well?

The freedom of the countryside is accorded to the foxhunter on a scale not allowed to anybody else. The walker is confined to the rights of way, the shooter to his woods and a little of the land around, but for the foxhunters nearly all is open, great spreads of thick hedged vale, rolling hills, army training grounds and locked demesnes, nearly all are open to you. There are few people who are so uncharitable as to deny access to hounds. Sometimes it is people slavishly devoted to shooting; Providence rewards them with hunting daughters. In our country we have a landowner who objects on humanitarian grounds, fine scruples that he overcomes annually in time to receive his shooting rents.

I like to combine as much sight-seeing with hunting as is possible: the parks of country houses are richly rewarding in this respect. I leave the hounds happily circling in thickets of laurel and search for ice houses, temples, boathouses and other luxuries of a former age. I remember one such place on the far side of our country that yielded not only a Grecian boathouse but a church on an island, a Victorian teahouse, a druidic megalith and a Roman road. I should add a note of caution to those who inspect boathouses on horseback; it is wise to have a sympathetic companion to hold the horse. Nor are the dull stretches of muddy vale so dear to the foxhunters devoid of interest. Our own is bisected by an enormous county boundary like a small Hadrian's Wall, covered with trees, snaking across the vale. In another place it is cleft by a dead straight and quite purposeless road that ends in a large bridge jumping a tiny brook, the whim of a nineteenth century eccentric. I do not think many of my fellow foxhunters share these interests, but the opportunities are there for those who care to look.

Foxhunters are often dismissed as a snobbish clique; this probably stems from the physical necessity for horsemen to look down on pedestrians and motorists, so it behoves the foxhunting fraternity to look down on people in as meek a manner as possible. I will not deny that there are people who take up the sport for reasons of a social nature. They imagine their stock will rise in the world's eyes and that opportunities will occur to meet their imagined betters; this may be the case, but a tumble or two levels the matter

THE CHASE

out. Foxhunting is a sport that crosses all social barriers, real or imagined, and a sociologist would be horrified to see his delicate house of cards tumble at the prospect of so much easy familiarity.

In the hunting field the eternal peacock can pirouette to his heart's content in a pink coat, a privilege shared only by circus ringmasters and holiday camp attendants. The detail and expense to which men (as opposed to women, who are second class citizens since they abandoned the side-saddle) can be put is limitless. To be perfectly dressed by the best London craftsmen can cost well over £1000. I would not advise the novice to embark on so extensive a sartorial voyage, as he would look foolish if his riding did not match his turnout: a muddy man in shabby clothes at 4.30 in the afternoon is more impressive than a pristine appearance at 11 o'clock in the morning. The work to maintain all this splendour is very considerable; it has in the first place to be made very sturdily so as to withstand not only damage in the field but the hour long brushing afterwards. The mystique of cleaning the BOOTS is a fine art in itself. For some people, the whole business has become more important than the hunting itself; their attentions naturally extend to the horse where there is a wealth of detail in saddlery and grooming. Our paragon arrives in the field exhausted by his labours and is quite unable to keep up, but I speak as one who is never tidy by nature.

I will not describe a really good hunt; the curious can turn to a copy of the 'Horse & Hound' or the novels of Surtees and Whyte-Melville. You do not have a good run every day: a large number of circumstances have to be exactly right. Firstly you need a good scent, whatever that is; an open country to ride across, preferably not too many people and, of course, a fox. The management of the hunt

THE DIVERSIONS

can guarantee most of these things except the scent about which is written and little known. If all these circumstances are present, a good run may be had and as a sporting experience, it can have few rivals. It is almost exclusively a participants sport which sadly limits the number of people who can experience it and these few, not being great propagandists, leave the glories unsung outside their immediate coterie. Luckily for the public at large, there is an emasculated variety of the sport available called racing in which all the unpredictable elements are removed.

There are certain drawbacks to the sport. It is expensive and time consuming and, try as you may to cut corners, there is no very cheap way. I have never resented the expense of the horse or the cost of the subscription to the hunt, it is the time spent at home fiddling with the brutes that is wasteful. I console myself with the thought that to have as many days shooting as I have hunting would be outrageously expensive, yet I envy the shooter as he cleans and cases his guns, out of mind and out of sight until the next day's sport. Time spent looking after the horse is thinning the ranks of the hunting farmers, the real support of the hunting field: good hunting country is often small dairy farming country and while the small dairy farmer makes a good living by hard work, he is desperately short of any time to enjoy that good living. My short cuts to save time are small things, like having brown nylon girths, a brown sheepskin under the saddle, these need less cleaning than their white equivalents, likewise a brown horse rather than a grey one, it all helps; nor need you make a fetish of grooming, plaiting the mane and tail and suchlikes, jobs that always need doing when you are in a hurry already.

Another difficulty is boredom; some people seem quite

THE CHASE

happy to sit around on horse back doing nothing, lucky they are to do so little and be content. I find these half hours interminably long and tedious. Hunting can also become dull if it becomes predictable. Our hunt has an excellent cover backed by a railway line and facing distant and extensive woods the other side of a couple of well hedged farms; each time we draw and find a fox the same brief but identical scurry occurs, we arrive at the edge of the woods, the huntsman blows his horn for his hounds while we stand around, like fishermen and their fish, exaggerating our leaps and chaffing each other. The uncertainties of the chase are its pleasures and with these gone, all is up.

One of the contradictions of the chase is that we who follow the sport are an homogeneous and consistent body of animal lovers; not only do we keep horses, but usually dogs, cats and sometimes budgerigars and goldfish, we keep them well and doubtless nurture fledglings and injured hedgehogs in season. Yet how can we reconcile this kindness with our bloodthirsty reputation? Some even say foxes enjoy being hunted; this I cannot believe as it can be frightening and uncomfortable keeping up with them in their flight, be you ever so well mounted and determined. The contradiction is solved by dismissing it without thought; an arbitrary solution to a knotty problem, not unlike the farmer who lovingly rears his farm stock only to send them to the slaughterhouse. In the country, life and death go side by side rather than one after the other. Should any qualms remain, a visit to a devastated poultry run will remind the undecided that our quarry is a vicious and unmerciful creature.

Fox hunting excites lively animosity in some portions of the community, ostensibly on the grounds that it is cruel, which it is; but these criticisms are overlaid with sentiments of a more general nature, a dislike of the haughty horseman who is suspected of being a 'better' or a survival of the bad old days. This animosity would increase except that large numbers of people think the sport dying or dead already and so not worth agitating about; I hope this is not true and am quite optimistic of the future. In the 1840's the railways were going to spoil it, in the 1900's it was barbed wire; my grandfather gave up the sport in the face of this threat, but his grandson gallops on. Greater threats are posed by the fragmentation of properties for, at the beginning of the century, the country I hunt in was the property of about twenty people excluding a few nests of sturdy freeholders who probably went hunting anyway. Many of these large landowners have disappeared entirely, foxhunting is not as fashionable as it was when it occupied a place in the fixed firmament of the late Victorian world alongside the Articles of Religion and $2\frac{1}{2}\%$ Consols, now we are beholden to so many people for favours and kindness. Innumerable people have to be visited; complaints, often very justified, have to be dealt with. Only two of the greater landlords support the hunt in any measure, only one of them still hunts and he is getting old. No longer can a single man defray the enormous expenses involved; the foxhunter of today has a great deal of homework to do to make his sport possible.

The sport is a magnificent, incongruous and romantic spectacle in an age of increasing drab uniformity. What continental farmer would tolerate a hundred horseman across his fields in an elated and dangerous frame of mind. If it is to be preserved, historical curiosity is reason sufficient and it is our duty to keep the panoply of the chase moving across the dull green winter fields of England: the rearguard action of a way of life and civilization supposedly on the wane but whose remnants are worth keeping.

Eleven
A Bloody Massacre

Once upon a time when a man wished to go shooting he would pick up his gun, collect the right sort of dog and walk off round his fields and woods, coming back some hours later with enough food for a couple of meals and declaring that he could eat them both, then and there. This is a very pleasant image of a sport at its best, Man in the raw; aided with an ingenious contrivance, namely a gun, doing a useful bit of foraging for his family. As I have said elsewhere, a man must hunt; our so-called civilization should not emasculate him by depriving him of this basic need. This happy state of affairs existed in the earlier part of the nineteenth century, marred only by draconian laws to protect the modest number of birds that existed naturally. What a lot of cricket the land-owning classes have had to play since in order to heal the divisive breach caused by over-keepering!

Now all is changed, enormous numbers of people wish to shoot enormous numbers of birds and the result is, in the words of a keen shooting friend, 'a bloody massacre'. Greed, technology and poultrymanship extort an unlimited number of birds from the smallest wood. In short, the sport has got out of hand. For we have arrived at a point of artificiality that fair bids to deprive shooting of its sporting qualities. For a sport to be a sport it must have one of two things but preferably both. These are exertion and

THE DIVERSIONS

risk and at the moment both have disappeared from pheasant shooting.

For those unaware of the system I will describe it briefly to show how far it has come from my ideal of the rough shooter. Young pheasant chicks are reared up to a reasonable age and enlarged in a sylvan poultry yard to grow on, defended by wire netting and electric fencing from their own foolishness and the foxes. This vast and sudden increase in so-called 'wild life' and their necessary food overheats the woodland economy, rats and mice abound near the corn feeders, likewise foxes who cannot resist the silly birds that have not learnt to roost up in trees. The pheasants eventually escape as they learn to fly and settle down in the nearby woods, the nearer the better as far as they are concerned being unadventurous creatures. Come the shooting season they are chased out of their bosky thickets by beaters and dogs, flying towards the guns. Some are shot, the unlucky ones fly on to land in the next wood to be drawn and are naturally reluctant to rise again because the pheasant is a heavy clattery sort of bird, easily exhausted by flight. Soon the dogs and beaters will urge them on out and up again. There has been nothing like it since the Romans and their arenas.

How is it that a fine sport has been turned into a bloody massacre? There are a lot of reasons, starting with the invention of the cartridge. In the days of muzzle loaders it took a minute to load your gun and so the sportsman was sparing and as certain as possible in his shooting. But the cartridge changed all that by making possible continuous firing. At about the same time the continental habit of driven game shooting came to England; no longer was our marksman happy to take the easy shot of a pheasant flying away; he could risk difficult birds directly above or even

A BLOODY MASSACRE

those approaching him; shots which in the days of the muzzle loader were not so easily achieved. I do not think we can put the clock back and drive out the driven bird, it is a greater test of marksmanship but it would be well to regard some of these foreign habits with suspicion; the French, for instance, shoot dicky birds; worse, the Italians eat them and all the while in the background is the plethoric German waiting for the roebuck to walk into his sights: their habits are indubitably suspect.

Another failing of the sport is that it has become more than fashionable; from once having been the occupation of a country gentleman it has now become a status bestowing sport. The newly enriched can appear passably like their more established brethren; for a modest sum compared to the freehold you can appear the territorial magnate: tweeds, Purdeys, keepers and all.

Not all landowners shoot but the demand is so great that any land can be let for the purpose and it brings in a welcome addition to estate income which cannot be disregarded; but the shooting tenants are sometimes so divorced from the life of the countryside that their manners and behaviour, passed on to the local inhabitants through their keepers, causes great offence. These men have paid good money and Heaven help anybody who goes near the scene of such expenditure. Large areas of land are locked up for half the year, hapless members of the public are shouted off the premises and much offence given. Unbeknown to the keepering profession, hand reared pheasants are not frightened of human beings; indeed they do not mind a bit of company at all and in my woods the job is done properly; all autumn hound puppies romp through the woods, hunting much more than their own Master would like, my lurchers chase rabbits, hare and deer and yet when the shooters come, the game is still there. They may blame the keepers or disturbance of the covers for bad sport but the principal cause of low bags is bad shooting and, need I add, for stirring birds up into some semblance of wild liveliness, there is nothing like a couple of visits from the hounds in September. Oh what a delicious heresy!

I shall also twit the shooting fraternity on the clothes they wear; the prevalence of rubber goods has driven out of the sporting field the marvellous twills and thorn-proofs that our grandparents wore. What a terrible creaking and rustling there is when a shoot assembles. How can they shoot in those waxed carapaces and india-rubber boots? The horrid truth is that the sport is so stationary that in wet weather, real water-proofing is obligatory, as are those walking sticks whose handles bifurcate to accommodate the sportsman's posterior.

Perhaps I have painted too gloomy a picture but the idea of a po-faced businessman, thoroughly water-proofed, armed with a second-hand Purdey, his only exercise jumping on and off a farm trailer between drives and paying hundreds of pounds for the privilege in the name of sport is ludicrous in the extreme.

There are, however, many better sides to the sport. Firstly there are those who shoot pigeons; this is useful vermin control and they are easy to pluck and good to eat: then there are those who shoot snipe and as I hold this impossible it is no mean achievement: there are those who shoot duck and get damp for their pains. The proper working of dogs is another sideline – I suspect it alleviates the boredom of interminable waiting. The foxhunter is allowed to do things beside his fellow sportsmen; guns cannot stand together for obvious reasons so a dog is the next best thing to a human but I would insist that they

A BLOODY MASSACRE

fall in with their owners wishes; who has not seen a cover spoilt by some unbiddable creature emerging at the wrong end surrounded by pheasants out of shot. When a dog and his owner are in perfect unison, it is a very fine sight.

Shooting is a farmers' sport par excellence and nowadays it does a farmer no harm at all to go for a bit of a walk: if they can afford to shoot, their farm business will have made them office bound. It is also very good value as the farm itself provides the woods and fields, the feed corn and much else. One farmer I know, now in his fifties and with active boys delighted to get on with the farm work, spends half the year keepering; indeed I believe he is more interested in that than the shooting itself. Another friend, author of the remark quoted earlier about 'a bloody massacre', who had been a keen prairie maker once, now plants trees and copses with as much enthusiasm as he destroyed them in his youth. Some parts of England, such as Norfolk and Suffolk, are saved only from perdition by woods kept as cover for game.

We have a shoot at home and I go out two or three times a season and all this slaughter occurs on my own ground despite my astringent observations earlier. The shooting is taken by a group of farming neighbours. They are good sorts to a man and I am only reconciled by the pleasure it seems to give them: they are numerous and noisy, their behaviour would raise eyebrows in East Anglia where these matters are taken seriously. They are not marvellous shots but at the end of the day there is a small surplus, some of which I take, being very fond of roast pheasant. The rest they divide up amongst themselves, each taking home a reasonable amount such as my ideal rough shooter would get. In this way I salve my conscience on the matter and can reserve my wrath for the 'hundred bird' man. Another acquaintance suffers very badly in this respect; his shoots are few and far between but the sky is darkened by clouds of pheasants and I am told, horror of horrors, that birds are let out of cages the night before into kale fields to achieve this spectacular effect. Oh you fat fousty man, may you be condemned in hell to walk your thousand acres on wet windy days with only a couple of cartridges and a hungry family at home!

Had I the time and the inclination I would contrive my shooting in a slightly different way. My guns (they would be the same farming neighbours mentioned earlier) would assemble and be divided into two halves. We would set off on foot for the first cover; on arrival one half would take up their positions outside and the other half would have the walking through, shooting only behind or directly above. At the next cover those who had not shot themselves or their friends would change places and so on throughout the day. There would be no use of little numbered tags for places; I would rely on the good nature of those who had shot well to give others a chance. This would eradicate competitive shooting for the game book as well as doing silly little sums. Everybody to do their own picking up and all dogs that misbehave to be left at home in future. There would be a great deal of walking: game would be left in certain places to be collected later and at the end of the day we would be much fitter and warmer than the sedentary shooter. Then and only then would we have a good square meal. This stern regimen would be a tall order for some but for me, a day's rough shooting with friends for a small bag far outweighs the pretentious artificiality of a grand battue with all the unwanted paraphenalia of beaters and keepers, tractors and cars, numbered stands and greedy competition.

Conclusion

When it comes to describing the cause of an affluent and privileged minority I feel much as a person would when campaigning for the reintroduction of corporal punishment in female penitentiaries. I cannot expect a great deal of sympathy from those less well off and as that includes nearly everyone in the country it is naturally imagined that this affluent minority can look after itself and needs no propagandist.

Landowners rely too heavily on their efficient pressure group, the Country Landowners' Association and when forced into the open repeat apologetic platitudes about the 'stewardship of the countryside' which are all very true but have been said too often. I will admit that there has been a tumble in standards since the time that Trevelyan describes in his book, a time when fox-hunting squires would bandy Latin tags as they flew their fences. For a start neither of these skills is considered to be of the slightest use or importance today; Latin is not heard in the hunting field and hunting itself is frowned upon as a cruel and iniquitous pursuit.

The main trouble in acting as a propagandist in this cause is that anything that smacks of elitism is now considered bad. The word elitist is a term of abuse amongst advanced political thinkers and I shall try to lay this bogey by observing that all societies have elites and the least

CONCLUSION

happy are those blessed with advanced political thinkers as rulers.

The first question asked is, 'Does our society need an elite and should that elite be of a rich and hereditary nature?' Being resigned, I hope, to the existence of elites, it is only a question of comparing the elites afoot and active today in various societies.

During this century various egalitarian experiments have been propagated outside this blessed isle (Thank the Lord). They are Utopian schemes of great ingenuity, based on a philosophy propounded by Karl Marx, a German of sorts, who, strange to relate, found this country the most congenial place to contrive his schemes. It is not for me to declare these experiments a success or otherwise, only to observe that they, too, have elites.

In many European countries the old elites, equivalent to our subject, have been totally destroyed by war and revolutions and such remains as survive have fossilized into introspective cliques, losing their purpose altogether. Spain maintains an old elite much like our own and this will be fortified now that the Crown as the fount of all honour has returned. By these comparisons it will be seen how lucky we are to retain our own elite, unsullied by revolution, still trying to be useful, having reasonably good manners and a respect for democratic institutions.

Because our old elite has lost much of its power, a secondary one has developed in this century which actually does the ruling. The two elites share the glory and the work in an amicable manner and occasionally trespass on each other's territory without causing offence. The vexatious or elderly members of the secondary elite can be immured without loss of credit in the historical confines of the older

CONCLUSION

elite; the House of Lords. All in all a marvellous example of our capacity for compromise.

And why, you may ask, should this elite be rich and enjoy many hereditary privileges? Human nature, being the deplorable thing it is, always puts by money and goods for future generations; such is the affection that parents feel for their children that they will go to any lengths to provide for them. Can such a natural urge be wrong? It would be most unwise to tamper.

To be of the elite is the object of ambitious people; the factory worker may not aspire to the ownership of a country estate but his managing director may well do so, and should he make the grade everybody beneath him takes a step up the ladder and there is a chance for the crowd at the bottom to set foot upon it. To view society as an interminable ladder covered with laborious climbers may seem a simplification, but it will suffice for our purposes and gives a fairer picture of the situation than the idea that the population is divided into just three classes. I would increase this number to some fifty million; the steps are consequently very gradual, the climb is not painful, even at times pleasant, and everybody can do a bit now and again in their spare time and be happy as a consequence. Nearly everybody is doing it; in business, the Civil Service and even under the umbrageous shade of some great levelling body like a Trade Union. The constant striving pervades all ranks and can be likened to a dog scratching for fleas, a powerful stimulant to that animal's well being and intelligence. So it is, if for no other reason, that there has to be a body of people seen to be enjoying life in an attractive manner. They need not be many or even ostentatious; that they are there is sufficient. Such is the carrot that draws on all the other donkeys in its train.

CONCLUSION

Now it so happens that people that have spent the best part of their lives successfully scuffling up the ladder will have some nasty habits by the time they get to the top. These are mainly concerned with money and its use, or an unfortunate manner towards those still climbing below. It is here that the hereditary principle can function with benefit. Our successful aspirant, freshly ennobled and enparked, will have a son who hopes to succeed to the results of his father's labours. He may not be a very satisfactory person because his father had too little time for him, but he may be free from his father's aggressive acquisitiveness and he, in turn, will have children who will be entirely untainted by what has gone before. This is how we arrive at our disinterested and incorruptible top layer of society. They may not be perfect but they will be free from an unhealthy preoccupation with worldly gain. Above all, they will have time; time to do things that are unprofitable, time to do things that others cannot afford to do, and time to start things that will never be finished in their own lifetime. It is this use of time that is the essence of civilization. It may not be the civilization of the eager enthusiast bent on improving the world with some irksome scheme, nor is it the beery heaven sometimes wrongly attributed to working people; it is a civilization that we have known and may even trust, it offers a certain 'douceur de vivre' that is not to be had elsewhere.

I will admit that it is unfair that some should be so lucky and others not, but there are two things to be remembered and should the envious experience them, their sentiments on the matter would be altered somewhat. One is the enormous amount of tax paid by this offensive minority, and I think it very rude to be unkind about the rich after they have paid their taxes. The second thing to be

CONCLUSION

remembered is the freezing discomfort of country houses in winter. I know no stronger recommendation for a cosy terrace house than that!

Despite the taxation and clammy houses there are still pockets of old-fashioned feudalism in England. Most people's knowledge of the landowning classes is drawn from a perusal of the novels of P. G. Wodehouse. These do not present an entirely faithful picture; scruffy old peers with a taste for pig-keeping doubtless still exist, but I am considering here the more normal hard-working landowner, as often as not without a peerage. You may be surprised when I say hard-working but this is often the case. It is commonly presumed that because a man need not work for his living, he does not. This is a fallacy fostered by novels and films that show an idealized rich living a life of dissipation in an atmosphere of studied luxury. This is the wishful thinking of those who know no better. To suspect the existence of a leisured class who do work is bitter medicine to many but I hope to show it useful even today.

To your true egalitarian, none of these arrangements has any value for we must all be ground to a very fine paste and then modelled anew. This process is so painful and expensive of human life and happiness that it can be dismissed out of hand. The slow progress of Russia can be held up as an example of the ensuing muddle that follows. Soon, however, we may emerge as the first country in and out of the industrial holocaust. By then our industrial inheritance will be sold for a mess of potage.

Increasing world population and diminishing negotiable food surpluses seem to indicate that this may happen literally and we will all be thrown back on the land. It is then that the landowners, if they have bothered to stay

CONCLUSION

around, will regain some of their early nineteenth century ascendancy. Should this happen it will be a good thing to have as many old hands as possible around, since they know the business so well. All this is very long-term stuff; the 'dark Satanic mills' have many years of work left in them and a more immediate use must be found for our landowners than running a 'back to the land' movement, tempting though the idea is.

At the moment, landowners are exploiting their past to great advantage; the taste for this past probably reflects the country's lack of confidence in the future, but it is not a bad sort of capital to work on for all that and large numbers of country houses are open to the public. Strongholds of aristocratic privacy are tumbling open in considerable numbers. The work suits the owners very well, gives employment in rural areas to lots of people too proud to be in service again and at the same time it reinstates the Big House in the neighbourhood. No longer is it a dilapidated white elephant with a palsied dowager huddled in a corner and hanging on. People's interests have widened and cavernous kitchens, teak sinks and hip baths are just as much appreciated as the Italian paintings upstairs whose country house ascriptions would not last fifty yards up Bond Street.

What strong thirst is being slaked? Are the visitors the meek of whom the Bible speaks, who, having inherited the earth, are trampling through the houses of their former masters in triumph, or are they people who have been missing their 'betters' subconsciously for years and have come to pay belated homage at the temples made new? I would like to think they were just curious and have time on their hands. There is a danger that their interest will make the stately showman feel obliged to enter into the act too whole-heartedly and act out a Wodehouse part, their flannel bags becoming preposterously amorphous, the leather patches on their tatty jackets overwhelming half the sleeve or more. There is a demand for this sort of stuff and nonsense, but it impairs a person's faculties and after a while the act takes over and leaves the human behind.

Another reason for preserving the landed interests is that they, in turn, preserve the countryside. Anyone who has lived anywhere decent looking, realizes that much of England is one great horrible 'wen' as Cobbett called it. No better instrument was ever contrived to prevent the spread of the awful than a wealthy landowner. This is because he is free from paltry temptations to knock down trees for cash, nor does he need to trim cottage gardens to make sites for bungalows, and while he may not be a man of taste himself, he has lived in decent surroundings and wishes to keep it that way.

The casual passer-by, driving down country lanes, may find the neighbourhood he is in very charming and before long he will pass the gates of a country house. Does he associate the two together? Probably not, and he drives on congratulating the work of the local planning authorities. But they are not the cause; committees never have taste – only anaemia. So it is that the best parts of England are the result of settled ownership. It is a small price to pay for such loveliness, the presence of an autocrat round the corner. Nor is his rule to be lightly dismissed as the 'dead hand of paternalism', for such a seemingly empty tract of farmland with quiet, tiny villages, are living rural communities free from encumbrances like some villages that are over-run with bungalows; (I have no objection to one-storey housing, only to the trappings about them), or senior citizens villages, full of gallant old majors reliving the

Normandy landings with bowsaws, in the orchards behind their cottages.

Another advantage of retaining a complete rural hierarchy is what I will call 'the freedom of the fields'; by this I mean that you and I can go for a walk without upsetting quite as many people as might otherwise be the case, for a man with ten thousand acres is unlikely to catch you trespassing and would have died long ago if he was upset every time it happened. Nor do his tenants feel so strongly because it is not their land. This division of responsibility is very advantageous in this respect but I do not want it to be taken as a permission to trespass because landowners still have a few foibles left, mainly to do with pheasants and horses.

These are my reasons for pleading the survival of a class of people that are considered by many to be an effete and powerless minority. The reasons may be specious and woolly, but since these people persist and are actually a very powerful minority on closer inspection, it is as well to look into their doings. Only a few years ago an archetypal specimen clambered in through a pantry window of No. 10, Downing Street, so we can presume that there is life in the old dog yet and this makes it a worthwhile subject for investigation. We are beginnig to realize that our society is not like a rotten-mouthed old man, all of whose teeth should be removed. Bits of society cannot be ruthlessly exorcised at the whim of the reformer. Dictators have done this with ease but have not often replaced the offending pieces with anything better.

The reader, even if he has borne with me this far, may find my approach to estate management too peculiar for his tastes; there are landowners who would not care to think themselves like the butcher and the baker, providing

CONCLUSION

a service to the community. On the other hand, to enjoy the respect of the neighbourhood on the grounds of wealth alone is but a further elevation of the worship of Mammon. All over England are properties run solely to make money, this being the only yardstick that the impoverished minds of the professional managers can grasp.

My attitude enables a landowner to identify himself with the community in which he lives, they are both part and parcel of the same thing, their interests are identical. When this is achieved the result is a balanced community in which a man can live in harmony with his neighbours despite the inevitable disparities of wealth and education and this is surely a strong defence against all the vagaries of man's making, be they political, egalitarian or ideological, that threaten to rend our world apart.